Evincepub Publishing

AF632384

Published by

Evincepub Publishing

Shivam Complex, Bilaspur, Chhattisgarh 495009

Ph.: +91-9171810321

e-Mail: publish@evincepub.com

Website: www.evincepub.com

First Edition: 2026

ISBN: 978-93-7335-287-9

MRP: ₹599/-

Publication Year: 2026

This book is also available on;

Amazon, Flipkart, Evincepub.com and Kindle

Communication Reimagined: Media, Technology & Society

Dr. Kaushik Mishra
Padmaja Tamuli

AUTHOR'S DETAILS

Sl. No.	Name of the Author	Designation & Affiliation
1	Dr. Sougand Akbarian	Assistant Professor, Islamic Azad University, Isfahan, Iran
2	Aditya Sharma	PhD Scholar, Department of Management Studies, AVB- IIITM Gwalior
3	Dr. Ananya Mehta	Associate Program Manager – Professional Communication & Senior Lecturer, RMIT University, Hanoi Campus, Vietnam
4	Koteshwar Ramesh Rakesh	Assistant Professor, Amity Institute of Psychology and Allied Sciences, Amity University, Noida, India
5	Dr. Shatabdi Som	Associate Professor, Amity School of Communication, Amity University, Kolkata
6	Sourav Manna	Senior Associate, Price water house Coopers (PwC), India
7	Mehakdeep Kaur	Soft Skills Trainer, Amity University Kolkata

8	Kaushik Roy	Research Scholar, University Institute of Media Studies, Chandigarh University, Chandigarh, Punjab, India
9	Dr. Chanchal Sachdeva Suri	Associate Professor, University Institute of Media Studies, Chandigarh University, Chandigarh, Punjab, India
10	Dr. Deepak Sharma	Assistant Professor, Amity School of Fine Arts, Amity University Kolkata, West Bengal
11	Mr. Indranil Bhattacharya	Assistant Professor, Amity School of Fine Arts, Amity University Kolkata, West Bengal
12	Mr. Sujit Kumar Karmakar	Assistant Professor, Amity School of Fine Arts, Amity University Kolkata, West Bengal
13	V Aswin	Junior Research Fellow, Dept. of Communication and Media Studies Bharathiar University, Coimbatore
14	Dr. M Srihari	Associate Professor, Dept. of Communication and Media Studies Bharathiar University, Coimbatore

CONTENTS

CHAPTER 1

Algorithmic Mediation of Culture and Language: Reconfiguring Meaning-Making in Digital Communication Ecosystems

Dr. Sougand Akbarian

Abstract: Digital, datafied, and algorithm-driven communication environments are reshaping how culture and language are produced, circulated, and interpreted. In platform-mediated societies, linguistic practices and cultural expressions are increasingly influenced by algorithmic curation, translational technologies, and globalized media flows. This chapter explores how these transformations affect meaning-making processes, particularly in Global South contexts where multilingualism and cultural hybridity are central. The study adopts a qualitative, interpretive approach based on critical discourse analysis and digital ethnographic insights drawn from existing interdisciplinary literature on media studies, sociolinguistics, and cultural communication. It examines selected cases of online communication practices across social media platforms, focusing on linguistic adaptation, code-switching, and cultural representation in algorithmically mediated spaces. Findings suggest that algorithmic systems do not merely distribute content but actively shape linguistic hierarchies and cultural visibility. Dominant languages, particularly global English, are amplified, while minority and regional languages are often marginalized or algorithmically deprioritized. However, users also resist and negotiate these structures through hybrid language use, creative translanguaging, and culturally embedded digital storytelling practices. The study highlights a dual process of homogenization and hybridization. While platform algorithms tend to standardize communication norms, they simultaneously enable new forms of cultural and linguistic innovation. This tension is particularly significant in multilingual societies, where identity, culture, and language intersect within digital infrastructures governed by opaque algorithmic logics.

Keywords: *Algorithmic communication, culture, language, digital media, multilingualism, translanguaging, Global South, platform studies, digital discourse, media and society*

1. Introduction

The rapid expansion of digital communication ecosystems has fundamentally transformed the ways culture and language are produced, circulated, and interpreted in contemporary societies. Social media platforms, artificial intelligence (AI)-driven recommendation systems, algorithmic translation tools, and datafied communication infrastructures increasingly mediate everyday interactions, shaping not only what users consume online but also how they express identity, culture, and linguistic belonging. In the twenty-first century, communication is no longer merely interpersonal or institutional; it is deeply platformized and algorithmically curated. Digital platforms such as TikTok, Instagram, YouTube, and X function as powerful cultural intermediaries that determine visibility, circulation, and relevance through opaque computational logics. These algorithmic systems influence the prominence of particular languages, narratives, and cultural representations while simultaneously marginalizing others (Couldry & Hepp, 2017; Gillespie, 2014).

Globalization and digital connectivity have intensified cross-cultural communication, enabling multilingual interactions across geographical and sociocultural boundaries. However, the rise of AI-driven communication technologies has also generated new forms of linguistic hierarchy and cultural standardization. Dominant global languages, particularly English, often receive algorithmic preference due to higher engagement metrics, data availability, and commercial value, thereby reinforcing existing inequalities within digital environments (Kwet, 2019). In multilingual societies of the Global South, where cultural hybridity and linguistic diversity are central to everyday communication, algorithmic mediation creates tensions between homogenization and local identity preservation. Users increasingly adapt their language practices to platform logics through code-switching, translanguaging, and hybrid digital expressions that blend local and global linguistic forms (Androutsopoulos, 2015).

This chapter examines how algorithmic communication systems reshape meaning-making processes in digital media environments, with particular attention to multilingual and culturally hybrid contexts in the Global South. The study investigates three central questions: How do algorithms shape linguistic visibility and cultural representation? How do multilingual users negotiate algorithmically mediated communication structures? What tensions emerge between cultural homogenization and hybridization within digital ecosystems? Employing a qualitative interpretive approach, the chapter draws upon critical discourse analysis and digital ethnographic insights from interdisciplinary scholarship in media studies, sociolinguistics, and cultural communication. By exploring the relationship between algorithms, language, and cultural representation, this study contributes to broader debates concerning digital power, platform governance, and the future of multilingual communication in increasingly algorithm-driven societies.

2. Literature Review and Theoretical Framework

The growing integration of algorithms into digital communication systems has transformed how language, culture, and identity are negotiated within contemporary media environments. Recent interdisciplinary scholarship in media studies, sociolinguistics, and digital humanities has increasingly focused on the role of algorithmic infrastructures in shaping communication practices, cultural representation, and linguistic visibility. Algorithmic communication refers to communication processes mediated, organized, and filtered through automated computational systems that determine what information users encounter online (Gillespie, 2014). Social media platforms and search engines rely on algorithms to curate content according to engagement metrics, personalization patterns, and commercial interests. These systems do not operate neutrally; rather, they shape public discourse by privileging particular narratives, languages, and cultural expressions while marginalizing others.

Platform studies scholars argue that digital platforms have become powerful sociocultural institutions that govern visibility and participation in online spaces (Van Dijck et al., 2018). Platforms such as TikTok, Instagram, and YouTube function not only as communication tools but also as algorithmically regulated ecosystems that influence cultural consumption and linguistic practices. The concept of "platformization" explains how social interactions, creativity, and cultural production are increasingly organized through platform logics driven by data extraction and monetization (Poell et al., 2019). These developments have profound implications for multilingual societies, particularly in the Global South, where digital participation occurs within unequal technological and linguistic structures.

Digital discourse studies further demonstrate how online communication reshapes traditional language practices. According to Norman Fairclough

(1995), discourse is closely connected to power relations and ideological structures. In digital environments, discourse becomes increasingly multimodal, participatory, and algorithmically influenced. Users adapt communication styles to platform affordances through hashtags, emojis, memes, abbreviations, and hybrid linguistic performances. The emergence of digital multilingualism has intensified practices of code-switching and translanguaging, where speakers fluidly combine multiple linguistic systems to negotiate identity and social belonging online (Androutsopoulos, 2015). Translanguaging challenges rigid boundaries between languages and reflects the dynamic communicative realities of multilingual users in digital spaces.

Theories of sociolinguistics and multilingualism are therefore essential for understanding algorithmically mediated communication. In multilingual digital ecosystems, language operates not only as a communicative resource but also as a marker of symbolic power and social capital. Pierre Bourdieu (1991) conceptualized language as a form of "linguistic capital" embedded within systems of power and social hierarchy. Within platform-mediated environments, dominant languages such as English possess greater algorithmic visibility because they align with global commercial markets and data infrastructures. Consequently, regional and minority languages are often algorithmically deprioritized, reinforcing linguistic inequality in digital communication. This dominance of global English has contributed to concerns about linguistic homogenization and cultural erasure in online spaces.

At the same time, scholars of cultural hybridity emphasize that globalization does not produce complete cultural uniformity. Stuart Hall (1997) argued that cultural identity is continuously constructed through representation and negotiation rather than fixed traditions. Similarly, Arjun Appadurai (1996) highlighted the complexity of global cultural flows through ethnoscapes, mediascapes, and ideoscapes that reshape local identities. Digital platforms facilitate hybrid forms of communication in which users combine local traditions, vernacular expressions, and global cultural symbols. These hybrid practices demonstrate that algorithmic communication environments simultaneously encourage standardization and creativity.

The concept of digital colonialism further deepens critiques of algorithmic communication. Scholars argue that global technology corporations exert disproportionate influence over knowledge production, communication infrastructures, and cultural representation in the Global South (Kwet, 2019). Digital colonialism describes how data extraction, platform governance, and AI systems reproduce historical inequalities between technologically dominant and marginalized regions. Algorithmic systems often privilege Western epistemologies, languages, and communication norms, thereby shaping whose voices become visible within global digital discourse. Such inequalities raise concerns regarding cultural autonomy, linguistic diversity, and epistemic justice in increasingly data-driven societies.

The theoretical framework of this study combines Critical Discourse Analysis (CDA), Platform Theory, Digital Ethnography, Cultural Hybridity Theory, and the concept of Linguistic Capital to examine algorithmic mediation in digital communication ecosystems. CDA, primarily associated with Norman Fairclough, provides a framework for analyzing how power relations and ideologies operate through language and discourse. This approach is particularly useful for examining how algorithms influence linguistic visibility and normalize dominant communication patterns online.

Platform Theory contributes to understanding the political and economic structures embedded within digital infrastructures. It enables analysis of how platform architectures and recommendation systems shape communication behaviors and cultural participation. Digital Ethnography complements this approach by examining users' everyday interactions within online communities and social media spaces. Through digital ethnographic observation, researchers can explore how multilingual users negotiate algorithmic constraints through translanguaging, code-switching, and hybrid identity performances.

Cultural Hybridity Theory, influenced by scholars such as Stuart Hall and Arjun Appadurai, provides insight into the fluid and negotiated nature of digital cultural identities. Finally, Pierre

Bourdieu's concept of linguistic capital explains how certain languages acquire symbolic and algorithmic value within platform economies. Together, these theoretical perspectives offer a multidimensional framework for understanding how algorithms shape language, culture, and meaning-making processes in contemporary digital ecosystems.

3. Methodology

This study adopts a qualitative and interpretive research design to examine how algorithmic communication systems shape language practices, cultural representation, and meaning-making within contemporary digital ecosystems. The research is grounded in an interdisciplinary framework that integrates perspectives from media studies, sociolinguistics, digital humanities, and cultural communication studies. Rather than focusing on quantitative measurement, the study emphasizes interpretive analysis of discourse, symbolic representation, and user interaction within algorithmically mediated online environments.

The primary methodological approach employed in this chapter is Critical Discourse Analysis (CDA), particularly informed by the work of Norman Fairclough (1995). CDA is used to investigate how language, power, and ideology operate within digital communication systems. This approach enables the study to analyze how algorithms influence linguistic visibility, normalize dominant communication patterns, and shape cultural narratives across digital platforms. The analysis focuses on the relationship between discourse practices and broader structures of technological and cultural power embedded within platform ecosystems.

In addition to CDA, the study incorporates elements of digital ethnography to examine everyday communication practices in online communities. Digital ethnographic observation allows for interpretive insights into how users negotiate platform logics through multilingual expression, translanguaging, code-switching, hashtag practices, meme culture, and culturally embedded storytelling. Observational examples are drawn from publicly accessible content and communication trends on major social media platforms, including TikTok, Instagram, X, and YouTube. These platforms were selected because of their global influence, algorithm-driven content distribution systems, and widespread use within multilingual and culturally diverse societies.

The study also relies on secondary interdisciplinary literature, including scholarly works on algorithmic communication, platform studies, multilingualism, cultural hybridity, and digital colonialism. Existing theoretical and empirical studies provide the foundation for interpreting contemporary digital communication practices within broader sociocultural and technological contexts.

Despite its analytical depth, the study has certain limitations. The research is primarily interpretive and does not include large-scale empirical data collection or computational analysis of platform algorithms.

Furthermore, platform algorithms are often opaque and continuously evolving, limiting the ability to fully examine their internal mechanisms. The selected examples are illustrative rather than exhaustive and may not represent all digital communication experiences across the Global South. Nevertheless, the qualitative methodology provides valuable insight into the complex relationship between algorithms, language, and cultural representation in contemporary digital societies.

4. Analysis and Discussion

4.1 Algorithmic Visibility and Linguistic Hierarchies

Digital platforms increasingly function as gatekeepers of linguistic visibility and cultural circulation. Algorithms embedded within social media ecosystems determine which forms of communication gain prominence, engagement, and monetization. Although these systems are often presented as neutral technological tools, they reflect broader political, economic, and linguistic hierarchies. One of the most visible outcomes of algorithmic mediation is the dominance of global English within online communication environments. Platforms prioritize content that generates higher engagement and broader marketability, which often advantages English-language content because of its global reach and advertising value (Gillespie, 2014).

Recommendation systems on platforms such as YouTube and TikTok tend to amplify languages associated with dominant digital economies. Content creators frequently adapt their linguistic practices to align with algorithmic expectations, employing English keywords, captions, and hashtags to increase visibility and engagement. This process resembles Search Engine Optimization (SEO)-style linguistic adaptation, where communication is strategically modified for algorithmic recognition rather than purely cultural or communicative purposes. Consequently, users in multilingual societies often experience pressure to privilege globally visible linguistic forms over local vernaculars.

The marginalization of regional and minority languages remains a significant issue in algorithmically driven ecosystems. Many AI-based translation and recommendation systems are trained predominantly on English-language datasets, leading to unequal technological support for non-dominant languages (Kwet, 2019). Regional languages may lack accurate translation tools, speech recognition systems, or algorithmic discoverability, reducing their digital visibility. In multilingual Global South contexts, creators using indigenous or regional languages often struggle to compete against English-dominated content streams. This dynamic reinforces what Pierre Bourdieu (1991) conceptualized as linguistic capital, where certain languages acquire greater symbolic and economic value within systems of power.

Algorithmic systems also normalize particular linguistic structures and communication styles. AI-driven translation technologies frequently standardize expressions according to dominant grammatical and cultural conventions, potentially erasing local idioms, dialects, and culturally embedded meanings. As a result, digital communication environments increasingly promote homogenized linguistic norms shaped by platform capitalism and datafication. Nevertheless, users continue to develop creative strategies to navigate and challenge these hierarchies through hybrid linguistic practices and digital cultural innovation.

4.2 Translanguaging and Hybrid Digital Identities

Despite pressures toward linguistic standardization, digital communication spaces also enable new forms of multilingual creativity and hybrid identity construction. Users actively negotiate algorithmic structures through translanguaging, code-switching, meme culture, and culturally hybrid digital performances. Translanguaging refers to the fluid use of multiple linguistic resources within a single communicative context, reflecting the dynamic realities of multilingual speakers rather than rigid separations between languages (Androutsopoulos, 2015).

On social media platforms such as Instagram and X, multilingual users frequently blend local languages with English to construct culturally layered identities. Hinglish, a hybrid combination of Hindi and English, has become a prominent mode of digital expression in India, particularly within memes, influencer culture, and youth communication. Similarly, Arabizi integrates Arabic and Latin script numerals in online communication, while Persian-English mixing reflects hybrid diasporic and transnational identities among Persian-speaking communities. These forms of communication demonstrate that multilingual users are not passive recipients of algorithmic structures but active participants in reshaping digital discourse.

Meme culture further illustrates the creative possibilities of hybrid communication. Memes often rely on multilingual humor, local references, and culturally specific linguistic adaptations that resist universal standardization. Regional hashtag cultures also enable users to organize digital communities around localized linguistic and cultural identities. Through hashtags in indigenous or regional languages, users create alternative spaces of visibility that challenge dominant algorithmic trends.

The emergence of hybrid digital identities aligns with Stuart Hall's (1997) understanding of identity as fluid, negotiated, and continuously reconstructed through representation. Digital communication environments encourage users to perform multiple identities simultaneously, combining global cultural symbols with local linguistic expressions. These practices reveal a complex tension between homogenization and hybridization. While algorithms favor standardized communication patterns for efficiency and marketability, users continually appropriate digital tools to preserve cultural specificity and linguistic diversity.

Moreover, translanguaging practices often function as forms of subtle resistance against linguistic hierarchies. By refusing strict adherence to standardized English, multilingual users assert local identity and cultural agency within global digital ecosystems. Such practices challenge the assumption that globalization necessarily produces cultural uniformity. Instead, digital communication becomes a contested space where users negotiate visibility, authenticity, and belonging through hybrid linguistic performance.

4.3 Cultural Representation and Platform Power

Algorithmic mediation significantly influences cultural representation within contemporary digital societies. Platforms operate through systems of visibility that determine which cultural narratives, aesthetics, and identities become globally recognizable. These processes are deeply connected to platform capitalism, where engagement metrics, advertising revenue, and data extraction shape cultural circulation (Van Dijck et al., 2018). As a result, algorithmic systems often privilege content aligned with dominant global trends while marginalizing localized or culturally specific expressions.

One consequence of this dynamic is cultural flattening, where diverse traditions and identities are simplified into globally consumable formats. Viral trends on platforms such as TikTok frequently encourage standardized aesthetics, musical styles, humor patterns, and communication behaviors. Influencer culture further reinforces these tendencies by promoting globally recognizable performances optimized for visibility and monetization. Local cultural practices are often adapted to fit platform-friendly formats, resulting in the commodification of identity and tradition.

The concept of digital colonialism provides a critical lens for understanding these inequalities. Scholars argue that large technology corporations exercise disproportionate control over digital infrastructures, communication systems, and cultural representation in the Global South (Kwet, 2019). Platform algorithms are primarily designed within Western technological and economic contexts, leading to the privileging of Western epistemologies, languages, and cultural norms. Consequently, the digital visibility of Global South cultures frequently depends upon their compatibility with dominant algorithmic standards.

This imbalance is particularly visible in AI-driven recommendation systems that amplify already popular or commercially viable content. Cultural narratives that align with dominant trends receive greater algorithmic exposure, while marginalized communities may remain underrepresented. As Michel Foucault suggested, power operates through systems of knowledge production and visibility. In digital ecosystems, algorithms function as mechanisms of cultural governance that shape public understanding of identity, authenticity, and social relevance.

However, cultural representation within digital spaces is not entirely controlled by platforms alone. Users actively reinterpret and localize global trends according to regional cultural contexts. This process reflects Arjun Appadurai's (1996) concept of global cultural flows, where local and global influences intersect dynamically rather than hierarchically. Digital communication ecosystems therefore remain spaces of both cultural domination and creative adaptation.

4.4 Negotiation, Resistance, and Digital Agency

Although algorithmic systems reinforce linguistic and cultural hierarchies, users continuously negotiate and resist these structures through acts of digital agency. Online communities employ counter-discourses, grassroots activism, and culturally embedded storytelling practices to reclaim visibility and challenge dominant narratives. These forms of resistance demonstrate that digital communication environments are not solely spaces of technological control but also sites of contestation and empowerment.

Grassroots digital activism has become particularly significant in multilingual and marginalized communities. Social media campaigns utilizing regional languages and indigenous narratives enable communities to preserve cultural memory and assert political visibility. Hashtag activism frequently mobilizes localized linguistic expressions to challenge dominant media representations and platform biases. Such practices create alternative publics where marginalized voices can circulate outside mainstream algorithmic priorities.

Community-building through digital storytelling also plays a crucial role in resisting homogenization. Indigenous creators and regional influencers increasingly use digital platforms to document oral traditions, local histories, and cultural rituals. On YouTube and Instagram, creators produce culturally specific content that reclaims linguistic identity and challenges assumptions about digital modernity. These practices illustrate how digital technologies can support cultural preservation as well as transformation.

Translanguaging and hybrid communication themselves function as forms of resistance. By combining global and local linguistic resources, users reject rigid linguistic hierarchies imposed by algorithmic systems. Multilingual expression becomes a strategy for maintaining cultural authenticity while participating in global digital culture. Such practices demonstrate that users are not passive subjects of platform power but active agents capable of reshaping digital communication norms.

Nevertheless, resistance within platform ecosystems remains constrained by algorithmic infrastructures and commercial logics. Alternative narratives often struggle for sustained visibility unless they align with engagement-driven platform metrics. This tension highlights the contradictory nature of digital communication ecosystems: they simultaneously enable cultural innovation and reinforce systemic inequality.

Ultimately, the relationship between algorithms, language, and culture is characterized by ongoing negotiation rather than technological determinism. Digital platforms shape meaning-making processes through systems of visibility and prioritization, yet users continuously reinterpret, resist, and transform these structures through creative linguistic and cultural practices. The coexistence of homogenization and hybridization reflects the complexity of communication in contemporary algorithmically mediated societies.

5. Conclusion

This chapter examined how algorithmically mediated digital communication ecosystems reshape language practices, cultural representation, and meaning-making processes in contemporary societies, particularly within multilingual contexts of the Global South. The analysis demonstrates that algorithms are not neutral technological tools; rather, they function as systems of cultural and linguistic governance that influence visibility, participation, and symbolic value within digital environments. Platform infrastructures and AI-driven recommendation systems increasingly determine which languages, identities, and narratives become prominent in online communication spaces.

One of the central findings of this study is the dual process of homogenization and hybridization operating simultaneously within digital communication ecosystems. On one hand, platform algorithms promote standardization by privileging globally dominant languages, particularly English, and by encouraging communication styles optimized for engagement, visibility, and monetization. Regional and minority languages frequently experience algorithmic marginalization, reinforcing existing linguistic and cultural inequalities. This dynamic reflects broader concerns regarding digital colonialism, platform capitalism, and the concentration of communicative power within global technology corporations.

On the other hand, the study also reveals the emergence of hybrid linguistic and cultural practices that challenge complete homogenization. Multilingual users actively negotiate algorithmic structures through translanguaging, code-switching, hybrid identity performances, and culturally embedded digital storytelling. Practices such as Hinglish, Arabizi, and Persian-English mixing illustrate how users creatively combine local and global linguistic resources to maintain cultural specificity while participating in transnational digital cultures. These forms of multilingual digital agency demonstrate that users remain active participants in shaping online discourse rather than passive recipients of algorithmic control.

The findings hold important implications for communication studies in the Global South. They highlight the necessity of examining digital communication through perspectives that recognize linguistic diversity, cultural hybridity, and unequal technological power relations. Future scholarship must continue investigating how algorithmic systems affect marginalized communities, indigenous languages, and local knowledge systems across diverse sociocultural contexts.

The chapter ultimately emphasizes the urgent need for more inclusive and ethically responsible algorithmic systems that support linguistic plurality and equitable cultural representation. Technology companies, policymakers, and digital researchers must address biases embedded within AI-driven communication infrastructures to ensure that digital spaces do not reproduce historical inequalities. Future research may further explore localized digital resistance practices, AI language governance, and the evolving relationship between multilingualism, identity, and algorithmic communication in increasingly datafied societies.

6. References

- Androutsopoulos, J. (2015). Networked multilingualism: Some language practices on Facebook and their implications. International Journal of Bilingualism, 19(2), 185–205. https://doi.org/10.1177/1367006913489198
- Appadurai, A. (1996). Modernity at large: Cultural dimensions of globalization. University of Minnesota Press.
- Bourdieu, P. (1991). Language and symbolic power. Harvard University Press.
- Couldry, N., & Hepp, A. (2017). The mediated construction of reality. Polity Press.
- Fairclough, N. (1995). Media discourse. Edward Arnold.
- Foucault, M. (1980). Power/knowledge: Selected interviews and other writings, 1972–1977. Pantheon Books.
- Gillespie, T. (2014). The relevance of algorithms. In T. Gillespie, P. J. Boczkowski, & K. A. Foot (Eds.), Media technologies: Essays on

communication, materiality, and society (pp. 167–194). MIT Press.

- Hall, S. (1997). Representation: Cultural representations and signifying practices. Sage.
- Kwet, M. (2019). Digital colonialism: US empire and the new imperialism in the Global South. Race & Class, 60(4), 3–26. https://doi.org/10.1177/0306396818823172
- Pink, S., Horst, H., Postill, J., Hjorth, L., Lewis, T., & Tacchi, J. (2016). Digital ethnography: Principles and practice. Sage.
- Poell, T., Nieborg, D., & Van Dijck, J. (2019). Platformisation. Internet Policy Review, 8(4), 1–13. https://doi.org/10.14763/2019.4.1425
- Van Dijck, J., Poell, T., & De Waal, M. (2018). The platform society: Public values in a connective world. Oxford University Press.

CHAPTER 2

AI-Assisted Spatial Interfaces: Behavioral Implications of Human–AI Interaction in AR Environments

Aditya Sharma

Abstract: While Augmented Reality (A.R.) gave richer contextual information to the users, the processing and interpretation of that data was left to the user. Given its ability to read surroundings and user requirements, as AI is embedded into AR interfaces it may begin to recommend action and guide users according to their needs. Though these characteristics improve efficiency while helping in decision making, there are concerns regarding how this guidance influences human behaviour. This chapter will discuss the impact of AI assisted spatial interaction upon human behaviour. This chapter documents how we moved from traditional AR systems that simply overlay digital data on the physical environment to AI-assisted AR systems that recognize context, assist a user personally and recommend action by analyzing how this may impact decision-making, user attention and exploration, cognitive load, trust and over reliance. The chapter also explores the roles of explainability, uncertainty communication and trust calibration in enabling effective human-AI interaction.

Keywords: *Augmented Reality; Artificial Intelligence; Human–AI Interaction; Human Agency*

1. Introduction

Traditionally, AR was focused on the visual addition of digital information to physical environments. The early systems helped to improve the perception of physical environments with an overlying layer of text, images and digital content (Azuma, 1997; Billinghurst et al., 2015). And they were mostly limited to information giving but the user was responsible for the interpretation of the information and attending to and making relevant actions.

More recently, AR has started to be merged with artificial Intelligence (AI), moving spatial interfaces away from being purely presentational. Navigations systems suggest pathways, applications support the maintenance of a facility prioritising certain components, retail interfaces highlight products based on relevant context and user behaviour. In other words the systems directly influences the user to interact with the environment (Devagiri et al., 2022).

As AI becomes embedded in spatial interfaces, there are deeper questions to be answered than just how well they work. Adaptive prompts, recommendations and guidance can reduce efforts and help users navigate complex information environments but at the same time they influence what information is noticed, which options are considered and how choices are considered. For example, a navigation system which continuously recommends optimal routes, may result in efficiency at the expense of an ability to explore independently. It is therefore not a matter of what AI assists useful, but how adaptive guidance shapes behaviour within spatial environments (Lee & See, 2004; Shneiderman, 2022).

AR is thus evolving from a medium for visual augmentation into a site of ongoing human-AI interaction, guidance, recommendation and adaptation actively shapes behavior. This chapter examines that transition by exploring the behavioral implications of AI-guided spatial interaction; the roles of trust and reliance in adaptive systems and design approached that support users without diminishing meaningful human agency.

2. From Spatial Visualization to AI-Mediated Interaction

Before considering how AI influences the behavioural dimensions of AI-guided spatial interaction, it is important to understand AR's evolution from a visualisation-based medium to something that is increasingly integrated with adaptive intelligence that influences interaction as it proceeds. The following sections outline this shift, from early representation-focused AR, to later systems with AI assisted spatial guidance while highlighting the changing role guidance in augmented environments.

2.1. Early AR as Spatial Visualization

Early AR systems were used to visualize digital information in the physical world. Digital information was superimposed over physical reality so that a user could remain aware of the spatial surrounding while gaining contextually relevant information (Azuma, 1997; Billinghurst et al., 2015). Examples included navigation cues, annotations and geo-visualization. This is evident in early research concerning AR to support human navigation and geo-visualization in which results show that AR based representations could help to access environmental information and enhance spatial awareness (Gardony et al., 2021).

Increasingly AR had been perceived through embodied interaction where users interact by moving through physical spaces and not all through what they look at. By immersing digital information within the real world, AR allowed for forms of exploration and learning in space that supported spatial cognition, memory and skill development (Jetter et al., 2014; Mania et al., 2006; Pacheco et al., 2015). However as technology grew early Augmented Reality Systems were more informational than adaptive, enriching perception and space representations, than adjusting to user behavior and influencing interaction.

2.2. AI-Assisted Spatial Interaction

Moving further ahead from simple information visualization, recent development of augmented reality combines concepts and advances from artificial intelligence, adaptive interfaces and context-aware computing to present content dynamically, reacting to user and task attributes and environmental parameters (Alvarez-Cortes et al., 2007) so that the user receives adaptive support is given while interacting than simply information being available.

AI is now used to recommend actions or prioritize information, add contextual prompts or adapt the content of the support information based on user and task (Meng et al., 2024). For example, a maintenance application might highlight parts of a system that it knows need inspecting, while a navigation application could continuously re-route directions so that these adapt to the movement of vehicles on congested one-way routes. So, AI becomes part of the interaction itself and controls what information users see and how task steps can take place.

Spatial Computing has accelerated this trend, bringing together the combination of digital content, physical context and adaptive intelligence in an interactive setting [REF: xuSpatial Computing Defining2024; liHuman Computer Interaction 2026]. This mimics patterns in other AI assistance interfaces that predict and reduce effort of information search by helping to streamline decision-making in other human-AI interfaces, e.g., AI Assisted Data Labeling (Desmond et al., 2021).

Unlike earlier AR systems, adaptive interfaces not only make information visible, they increasingly recommend, prioritize and shape interaction. With that the central question changes from what you see in the augmented environment to how AI influences your behavior within it.

3. Behavioral Implications of AI-Guided Spatial Interaction

Given that adaptive systems recommend actions, direct attention and filter information, the shift from pure information visualization towards AI-assisted spatial interaction has greater behavioral consequences. Such systems play an active role in how people engage with their surroundings and exploring this effect means to consider what effect AI guidance will have on decision making, attention, exploration, cognitive offloading and levels of autonomy when interacting within AR environments.

3.1. AI Guidance and Spatial Decision-Making

The integration of AI into spatial interfaces has made decision making, in part mediated by the system generated suggestions, than merely user interpretation. In navigation and guidance applications this influence is highly evident. AR systems can make recommendations on routes; highlight environmental features or direct attention toward particular locations depending on contextual information. Research indicates that positioning guidance cues within a user's field of view has an impact on navigation behavior by influencing attention between the digital information and the surrounding environment (S. Wang et al., 2025). The guidance impacts not only the decision but also the way other options are perceived and evaluated.

Similar characteristics can be seen within contextual prompts or adaptive recommendations, such as adaptive overlays to direct focus in industrial maintenance or route recommendations dynamically updated by a navigation system. Such prompts reduce search effort help users focus on information that appears most relevant (Alvarez-Cortes et al., 2007; Meng et al., 2024).

Guidance is, however, rarely neutral. Spatial cues strongly determine what users notice, what alternatives are considered and how surrounding is interpreted. Studies of attention steering mechanisms in AR suggest that the cues shown in system's interfaces not only focus attention on selected user and task targets but modify responses and decision behaviour arising from viewing, shaping how users engage with physical environments themselves and blurring the line between spatial interface and personal, unguided decision of participants or actors using any such system (Rusch et al., 2013; Wolf et al., 2023)

3.2. Attention, Exploration, and Cognitive Offloading

And since, adaptive AR systems drive attention towards selected objects, locations through visual cues, recommendations and prompts, it impacts what the user sees and does not see (Wolf et al., 2023). Therefore, these cues themselves can be not simply for information purposes but for perception purposes as well. This can be beneficial for situations where you need to process information faster like navigating during emergency situations so the user gets directed towards most important areas (Rusch et al., 2013).

Then there are several questions of exploration and discovery. When navigating unfamiliar environments, users, generally, move through unknown territory, by marking landmarks, alternative routes options. Though ai-guided system provide recommendations that help focus attention to selected information which might increase effectiveness, but it can decrease explorative behaviour because the systems take away the need to seek information from the users. Such attentional tunneling was observed in AR, when some important cues made users focus only on their target, while being less aware about unexpected information which may be important (Dixon et al., 2013).

These discussed topics are closely related to cognitive offloading. Many people tend to rely on external tools to reduce memory load, monitoring load or decision load, whenever a task is complicated or their attention is divided over multiple parallel actions (Wahn et al., 2023; Weis & Wiese, 2019a). In AR systems recommendations, reminders, visual cues or filtered information helps users to process environmental information efficiently. This frees cognitive resources and generally enhances the primary task performance (Diaz Alfaro et al., 2024; Grinschgl et al., 2023). Nonetheless, increasing reliance on system generated information changes the interactions of users with the environment and opens questions about how long-term behaviour changes due to adaptive guidance.

3.3. Assistance, Autonomy, and Behavioral Tensions

As the usage of ai guidance increases in AR interfaces, it introduces a central behaviour tension about balance between assistance and human agency. On one hand, adaptive systems increase efficiency, reduce cognitive effort and empower users in decision-making in complex environments while on the other, increases dependence on system-generated guidance at the expense of user choice and autonomy and it remians doubtful whether interaction with the system is more self-initiated or system-initiated. The question in not whether assistance is a positive thing, that is self-evident, but rather how reliance on system guidance alters the users own reliance on their cognitive processes. Research on cognitive offloading suggests individuals are motivated to delegate memory retention, monitoring and decision-support to external systems if it reduces effort or increases performance (Hamilton & Yao, 2018; Weis & Wiese, 2019a), in the case of AI assisted AR technologies this may be in the form of system recommended navigations, contextual prompts, filtering of information or adaptable guidance which is a necessary especially when an individual's own attentional resources may be under strain, further extending cognition during the course of human-machine interaction (Diaz Alfaro et al., 2024; Wahn et al., 2023).

Reliance on adaptive guidance is influenced not only by task demands but also by the perceived reliability and trustworthiness of systems. Generally users are more open to delegate cognitive tasks when they think systems are reliable and can be trusted (Peng & Yeh, 2025; Weis & Wiese, 2019b). As trust in adaptive guidance increases, the individual's scrutiny of recommendations decreases which leads to recommendations playing a greater role in decision making. This shift in the balance between independent judgment and system led decision making can occur over time.

This does not mean that every consequence is negative. Cognitive support may improve workload and performance, but the problem lies in the fact that when assistance becomes too easy, opportunities for independent reasoning, exploration or skill development are eliminated. Similar concerns about de-skilling and over-reliance have been raised when discussing AI-assisted work due to repeated dependence on automated support, as it may reduce one's active engagement with a task (Shukla et al., 2025). Over time such patterns may develop where users are used to follow recommendations than to evaluate alternatives themselves.

Therefore, the issue is not to eliminate AI guidance totally, but how this assistance can be balanced with agency so that AI assisted spatial interfaces become cognitive partners that support spatial exploration than diminish opportunities for cognitive deliberation, self examination & independent decision making (García-Barrios, 2025).

4. Trust, Reliance, and Interpretation in Adaptive AR Systems

The behavioral effects of AI-guided spatial interaction are directly linked to how users understand and rate system guidance, as adaptive recommendations can only affect behavior should the user decide to place their trust in the system. Therefore, trust and interpretation are central for effective human-AI interaction. This section will discuss the importance of trust, reliance, mental models, explainability and uncertainty communication with respect to AI guidance within AR environments.

4.1. Trust and Reliance in AI-Assisted Interaction

As AI-assisted spatial interfaces increasingly guide attention within dynamic environments, actively recommending actions and prioritizing information, it is important for users to continuously evaluate whether the recommendations are trustworthy. Effective interaction, therefore, relies as much on users' willingness to trust the assistance as it does on system performance. Trust in adaptive guidance emerges from repeated interaction. When the suggestions from adaptive AR interfaces consistently lead to useful outcomes, it makes the users more confident with their recommendations over time. An AR navigation interface repeatedly identifying optimal routes, can help build a confident expectation of reliability. Trust, therefore, builds through continuous repeated experience with system behaviors rather than from the mere presence of AI assistance (Dzindolet et al., 2003).

However, reliance depends on more than just trust in the system. For example, users consider factors like overall risk evaluation, situational demands and the consequences if the suggestion fails. In situations or environments with low-stakes, AI suggestions will mostly be accepted without much scrutiny, whereas in high-stakes environments, recommendations may not only receive attention but also intense scrutiny (Solberg et al., 2022). So we can say that the relation between trust and reliance is dynamic, not fixed.

These dynamics reinforce the significance of trust calibration. This means that effective human–AI interaction does not require trusting unconditionally, but in line with the true capabilities of the system. Excessive trust will lead to acceptance of even questionable recommendations while too little trust will lead to ignoring valuable guidance. So, reliance is most effective when users adjust their confidence in response to changing system performance and communicated uncertainty (Marusich et al., 2025; Okamura & Yamada, 2020).

4.2. Explainability, Uncertainty, and Human Interpretation

However, trust alone does not decide AI's level of impact on user decision. Users have to interpret recommendations, infer their plausibility and decide how much guidance they should receive during decision making. This process is particularly important in adaptive AR environments, where recommendations are delivered in real time and embedded within ongoing activities like evaluating an alternative route, users have to decide if they should follow the recommendations. These decisions show users' mental models for these AI systems like how it works, and what are its limitations (Gero et al., 2020).

Explainability plays an important role here as it allows users to understand motivations for recommendations against observable aspects of a particular task or environment. Explainability does not, however, lead to better decision making and sometimes encourages participants to over-rely on AI advice irrespective of the accuracy or certainty being provided (Naiseh et al., 2021). The same effect is identified about the use of certainty - participants adjust to the receipt of information about the uncertainty and reliability of an AI more readily if communicated in understandable and actionable terms (Marusich et al., 2025; Tomsett et al., 2020). Rather than trying to replace human interpretation, these interventions give the user guidance on when to rely on AI or when to seek additional information. Trust, interpretation and reliance are intrinsically connected to each other and it is through the ongoing negotiation of these that humans and AI communicate in an adaptive spatial environment.

5. Designing Constraint-Aware Spatial AI Systems

The behavioural and cognitive effects of AI guidance in interaction have strong consequences for system design. As adaptive AR systems influence attention, decision-making, trust and reliance, the challenge is not only how to improve technical performance, but also about the way guidance is delivered, interpreted and integrated into the activity system. In this section we introduce key cognitive and interaction constraints during adaptive AR and discuss how spatial AI systems can balance providing effective assistance with human agency.

5.1. Cognitive and Interaction Constraints in Adaptive AR

The advantages of AI-enhanced spatial interaction are balanced by cognitive and interaction constraints that influence user performance and experience. Although adaptive recommendations aim to reduce effort and help decision-making, all the recommendations, explanations and visual overlays provided might impose demands on the user's attention. With AI systems becoming more active in the spatial environment, the goal is not just to provide assistance but to do so in ways that it remains cognitively manageable.

One concern includes cognitive overload. While adaptive systems can filter and highlight relevant information, thereby simplifying a task, users still have to process multiple recommendations or resolve conflicts while continuing other tasks (Yao et al., 2026). In environments where attention is divided among digital content and physical surroundings, more information does not necessarily improve performance.

Other challenges can include attention fragmentation and information overburden. AR puts information right in the field of view of the user and give information fast, but numerous prompts, notifications or explanation might overload a user's limited cognitive attention. When transparency mechanisms offer information beyond a user's capacity during interaction, it become a cognitive load than a help (Herm, 2023).

Adaptive systems too have challenges in vigilance and consistency. If AI provides robust recommendations over time, the users show complacency in verifying the details (Zhao et al., 2024), while when there is inconsistency in system behavior, then responses change in ways a user cannot anticipate thus trust and reliability suffers. It is important for a system to take care of cognitive limit of the user than to just strive for more assistance. More does not automatically mean better.

5.2. Balancing Adaptive Assistance and Human Agency

These constraints highlight the need to strike a balance between providing adaptive assistance and maintaining human autonomy. The aim of an AI-assisted spatial interface should not be to simply maximize automation, but to improve the user' s capabilities, keeping the user meaningfully involved throughout the decision-making process. This balance is particularlty important in an AR application since many suggestions occur directly within ongoing activities.

One way to help strike this balance is to make users aware of both his current surroundings and role of the AI within the interface. Preserving situation awareness can ensure that users act as active decision makers, than passively accepting suggestions from AI (Jiang et al., 2023). Understanding task context and basis of system guidance promotes critical evaluation of AI recommendations and allows the human to intervene and correct the AI suggestions when necessary.

The design of adaptive assistance can also affect control perception. Explanations can promote understanding and collaboration, but its effectiveness depends on the timing, complexity and degree of system autonomy (Hauptman et al., 2024; B. Wang et al., 2024). Excessive explanations may add a higher cognitive burden, whereas insufficient explanations can leave them wanting for more. Effective assistance means explanation strategies that support decision-making without overwhelming the users.

Although automation has many benefits, a single level of automation does not apply across all user situations, tasks or environments. Research on situational autonomy suggests that adaptive systems often perform most effectively when assistance levels adjust to context rather than remain fixed (Salikutluk et al., 2024). Systems that preserve opportunities for oversight and intervention can help maintain trust, control, and situation awareness even when adaptive guidance is actively provided (Calhoun, 2022).

Constraint-aware spatial AI is not so much defined by the amount of assistance available but at how well it mediates that assistance with human judgement; that guidance should be available without overriding and adaptive without becoming unpredictable.

6. Future Research Directions

The growing integration of AI into spatial interfaces raises questions that remain insufficiently understood. Existing research has largely focused on task performance, usability, and short-term user responses, with less attention given to the long-term effects of adaptive guidance. As AI-mediated recommendations become embedded within activities such as navigation, learning, maintenance, and information seeking, future research should examinc how repeated interaction shapes decision-making habits, exploration behaviors, and reliance on adaptive support.

There is also a need for evaluation approaches that extend beyond traditional performance measures. Improvements in efficiency may not fully capture the broader behavioral consequences of adaptive guidance. Future studies should therefore examine outcomes such as autonomy, trust calibration, attention allocation, and independent judgment.

Another important direction concerns explainable spatial guidance. Although explainability has received considerable attention in human–AI interaction research, less is known about how explanations should be presented within dynamic AR environments. Understanding how transparency and uncertainty can support user interpretation without disrupting interaction remains an important challenge.

More broadly, future research should continue exploring how adaptive assistance can be balanced with human agency as AI assumes a more active role in shaping behavior within physical environments.

7. Conclusion

Augmented reality is evolving beyond its traditional role as a visualization technology. As AI capabilities become integrated into spatial interfaces, adaptive systems increasingly recommend actions, guide attention, filter information, and provide context-sensitive support. This shift transforms AR into a setting for ongoing human–AI interaction and raises important questions regarding decision-making, exploration, cognitive offloading, trust, and reliance.

The central challenge emerging from this transition concerns the balance between guidance and agency. AI-assisted spatial interfaces can reduce cognitive demands and support users in complex environments, but effective interaction depends on preserving opportunities for independent judgment, exploration, and control.

Designing human-centered spatial AI systems therefore requires more than increasingly sophisticated guidance. It requires careful consideration of how assistance is introduced, interpreted, and relied upon in practice. The long-term success of AI-assisted spatial environments will depend on how effectively they enhance performance while preserving meaningful human agency.

References

- Alvarez-Cortes, V., Zayas-Perez, B. E., Zarate-Silva, V. H., & Ramirez Uresti, J. A. (2007). Current trends in adaptive user interfaces: Challenges and applications. *Electronics, Robotics and Automotive Mechanics Conference (CERMA 2007)*, 312–317. https://doi.org/10.1109/CERMA.2007.4367705
- Azuma, R. T. (1997). A survey of augmented reality. *Presence: Teleoperators and Virtual Environments,* *6*(4), 355–385. https://doi.org/10.1162/pres.1997.6.4.355
- Billinghurst, M., Clark, A., & Lee, G. (2015). A survey of augmented reality. *Foundations and Trends in Human–Computer Interaction, 8*(2–3), 73–272. https://doi.org/10.1561/1100000049
- Calhoun, G. (2022). Adaptable (not adaptive) automation: Forefront of human–automation teaming. *Human Factors, 64*(2), 269–277. https://doi.org/10.1177/00187208211037457
- Desmond, M., Muller, M., Ashktorab, Z., Dugan, C., Duesterwald, E., Brimijoin, K., Finegan-Dollak, C., Brachman, M., Sharma, A., Joshi, N. N., & Pan, Q. (2021). Increasing the speed and accuracy of data labeling through an AI-assisted interface. In *Proceedings of the 26th International Conference on Intelligent User*

Interfaces (pp. 392–401). https://doi.org/10.1145/3397481.3450698

- Devagiri, J. S., Paheding, S., Niyaz, Q., Yang, X., & Smith, S. (2022). Augmented reality and artificial intelligence in industry: Trends, tools, and future challenges. *Expert Systems with Applications, 207*, 118002. https://doi.org/10.1016/j.eswa.2022.118002
- Diaz Alfaro, G., Fiore, S. M., & Oden, K. (2024). Externalized and extended cognition: Cognitive offloading for human-machine teaming. *Proceedings of the Human Factors and Ergonomics Society Annual Meeting, 68*(1), 290–293. https://doi.org/10.1177/10711813241275506
- Dixon, B. J., Daly, M. J., Chan, H., Vescan, A. D., Witterick, I. J., & Irish, J. C. (2013). Surgeons blinded by enhanced navigation: The effect of augmented reality on attention. *Surgical Endoscopy, 27*(2), 454–461. https://doi.org/10.1007/s00464-012-2457-3
- Dzindolet, M. T., Peterson, S. A., Pomranky, R. A., Pierce, L. G., & Beck, H. P. (2003). The role of trust in automation reliance. *International Journal of Human–Computer Studies, 58*(6), 697–718. https://doi.org/10.1016/S1071-5819(03)00038-7
- García-Barrios, D. A. (2025). Epistemic partner or cognitive crutch: A conceptual model of cognitive offloading in human–artificial intelligence collaboration. *IEEE Internet*

Computing, 29(5), 7–16. https://doi.org/10.1109/MIC.2025.3626694

- Gardony, A. L., Martis, S. B., Taylor, H. A., & Brunyé, T. T. (2021). Interaction strategies for effective augmented reality geo-visualization: Insights from spatial cognition. *Human–Computer Interaction, 36*(2), 107–149. https://doi.org/10.1080/07370024.2018.1531001

- Gero, K. I., Ashktorab, Z., Dugan, C., Pan, Q., Johnson, J., Geyer, W., Ruiz, M., Miller, S., Millen, D. R., Campbell, M., Kumaravel, S., & Zhang, W. (2020). Mental models of AI agents in a cooperative game setting. In *Proceedings of the 2020 CHI Conference on Human Factors in Computing Systems* (pp. 1–12). https://doi.org/10.1145/3313831.3376316

- Grinschgl, S., Papenmeier, F., & Meyerhoff, H. S. (2023). Mutual interplay between cognitive offloading and secondary task performance. *Psychonomic Bulletin & Review, 30*(6), 2250–2261. https://doi.org/10.3758/s13423-023-02312-3

- Hamilton, K. A., & Yao, M. Z. (2018). Cognitive offloading and the extended digital self. In M. Kurosu (Ed.), *Human-computer interaction: Theories, methods, and human issues* (Vol. 10901, pp. 257–268). Springer International Publishing. https://doi.org/10.1007/978-3-319-91238-7_22

- Hauptman, A. I., Schelble, B. G., Duan, W., Flathmann, C., & McNeese, N. J. (2024).

Understanding the influence of AI autonomy on AI explainability levels in human-AI teams using a mixed methods approach. *Cognition, Technology & Work, 26*(3), 435–455. https://doi.org/10.1007/s10111-024-00765-7

- Herm, L.-V. (2023). Impact of explainable AI on cognitive load: Insights from an empirical study. *arXiv*. https://doi.org/10.48550/arXiv.2304.08861

- Jetter, H.-C., Reiterer, H., & Geyer, F. (2014). Blended interaction: Understanding natural human–computer interaction in post-WIMP interactive spaces. *Personal and Ubiquitous Computing, 18*(5), 1139–1158. https://doi.org/10.1007/s00779-013-0725-4

- Jiang, J., Karran, A. J., Coursaris, C. K., Léger, P.-M., & Beringer, J. (2023). A situation awareness perspective on human-AI interaction: Tensions and opportunities. *International Journal of Human–Computer Interaction, 39*(9), 1789–1806. https://doi.org/10.1080/10447318.2022.2093863

- Lee, J. D., & See, K. A. (2004). Trust in automation: Designing for appropriate reliance. *Human Factors, 46*(1), 50–80. https://doi.org/10.1518/hfes.46.1.50_30392

- Mania, K., Wooldridge, D., Coxon, M., & Robinson, A. (2006). The effect of visual and interaction fidelity on spatial cognition in immersive virtual environments. *IEEE Transactions on Visualization and Computer*

Graphics, 12(3), 396–404. https://doi.org/10.1109/TVCG.2006.55

- Marusich, L. R., Files, B. T., Bancilhon, M., Rawal, J. C., & Raglin, A. (2025). Trust calibration for joint human/AI decision-making in dynamic and uncertain contexts. In H. Degen & S. Ntoa (Eds.), *Artificial intelligence in HCI* (Vol. 15819, pp. 106–120). Springer Nature Switzerland. https://doi.org/10.1007/978-3-031-93412-4_6

- Meng, S., Dollahite, R., Kaur, A., Schell, P., Sharma, A., Ventre, G., Kranz, I., Nudelman, G., & Gerling, G. J. (2024). Developing design features to facilitate AI-assisted user interactions. In *Proceedings of the 2024 Systems and Information Engineering Design Symposium (SIEDS)* (pp. 437–442). https://doi.org/10.1109/SIEDS61124.2024.10534665

- Naiseh, M., Al-Thani, D., Jiang, N., & Ali, R. (2021). Explainable recommendation: When design meets trust calibration. *World Wide Web, 24*(5), 1857–1884. https://doi.org/10.1007/s11280-021-00916-0

- Okamura, K., & Yamada, S. (2020). Empirical evaluations of framework for adaptive trust calibration in human-AI cooperation. *IEEE Access, 8*, 220335–220351. https://doi.org/10.1109/ACCESS.2020.3042556

- Pacheco, D., Wierenga, S., Omedas, P., Oliva, L. S., Wilbricht, S., Billib, S., Knoch, H., &

Verschure, P. F. M. J. (2015). A location-based augmented reality system for the spatial interaction with historical datasets. In *2015 Digital Heritage* (pp. 393–396). https://doi.org/10.1109/DigitalHeritage.2015.7413911

- Peng, J.-L., & Yeh, S.-L. (2025). Cognitive offloading in short-term memory tasks: Trust toward tools as a moderator. *International Journal of Human–Computer Interaction, 41*(21), 13382–13393. https://doi.org/10.1080/10447318.2025.2474449

- Rusch, M. L., Schall, M. C., Gavin, P., Lee, J. D., Dawson, J. D., Vecera, S., & Rizzo, M. (2013). Directing driver attention with augmented reality cues. *Transportation Research Part F: Traffic Psychology and Behaviour, 16*, 127–137. https://doi.org/10.1016/j.trf.2012.08.007

- Salikutluk, V., Schöpper, J., Herbert, F., Scheuermann, K., Frodl, E., Balfanz, D., Jäkel, F., & Koert, D. (2024). An evaluation of situational autonomy for human-AI collaboration in a shared workspace setting. In *Proceedings of the CHI Conference on Human Factors in Computing Systems* (pp. 1–17). https://doi.org/10.1145/3613904.3642564

- Shneiderman, B. (2022). Human-centered AI. In *Proceedings of the 5th Workshop on Human Factors in Hypertext* (pp. 1–2). https://doi.org/10.1145/3538882.3542790

➢ Shukla, P., Bui, P., Levy, S. S., Kowalski, M., Baigelenov, A., & Parsons, P. (2025). De-skilling, cognitive offloading, and misplaced responsibilities: Potential ironies of AI-assisted design. In *Proceedings of the Extended Abstracts of the CHI Conference on Human Factors in Computing Systems* (pp. 1–7). https://doi.org/10.1145/3706599.3719931

➢ Solberg, E., Kaarstad, M., Eitrheim, M. H. R., Bisio, R., Reegård, K., & Bloch, M. (2022). A conceptual model of trust, perceived risk, and reliance on AI decision aids. *Group & Organization Management, 47*(2), 187–222. https://doi.org/10.1177/10596011221081238

➢ Tomsett, R., Preece, A., Braines, D., Cerutti, F., Chakraborty, S., Srivastava, M., Pearson, G., & Kaplan, L. (2020). Rapid trust calibration through interpretable and uncertainty-aware AI. *Patterns, 1*(4), 100049. https://doi.org/10.1016/j.patter.2020.100049

➢ Wahn, B., Schmitz, L., Gerster, F. N., & Weiss, M. (2023). Offloading under cognitive load: Humans are willing to offload parts of an attentionally demanding task to an algorithm. *PLOS ONE, 18*(5), e0286102. https://doi.org/10.1371/journal.pone.0286102

➢ Wang, B., Yuan, T., & Rau, P.-L. P. (2024). Effects of explanation strategy and autonomy of explainable AI on human-AI collaborative decision-making. *International Journal of Social*

Robotics, 16(4), 791–810. https://doi.org/10.1007/s12369-024-01132-2

- Wang, S., Xu, Q., & Schoeffmann, K. (2025). Exploring the effects of augmented reality guidance position within a body-fixed coordinate system on pedestrian navigation. *IEEE Transactions on Visualization and Computer Graphics, 31*(11), 9921–9931. https://doi.org/10.1109/TVCG.2025.3616773

- Weis, P. P., & Wiese, E. (2019a). Problem solvers adjust cognitive offloading based on performance goals. *Cognitive Science, 43*(12), e12802. https://doi.org/10.1111/cogs.12802

- Weis, P. P., & Wiese, E. (2019b). Using tools to help us think: Actual but also believed reliability modulates cognitive offloading. *Human Factors, 61*(2), 243–254. https://doi.org/10.1177/0018720818797553

- Wolf, J., Luchmann, D., Lohmeyer, Q., Farshad, M., Fürnstahl, P., & Meboldt, M. (2023). How different augmented reality visualizations for drilling affect trajectory deviation, visual attention, and user experience. *International Journal of Computer Assisted Radiology and Surgery, 18*(8), 1363–1371. https://doi.org/10.1007/s11548-022-02819-5

- Yao, Y., Han, T., & Li, D. (2026). Assistance or distraction? A cognitive ergonomics perspective on cognitive load during AI-assisted post-editing. *International Journal of Human–*

Computer Interaction, 1–20. https://doi.org/10.1080/10447318.2026.2628994

- Zhao, C., Qu, B., Zhou, J., & Lin, C. (2024). The effect of AI-induced outcome favorability on vigilance performance: An exploration based on attention capacity theory. *Current Psychology, 43*(13), 11493–11506. https://doi.org/10.1007/s12144-023-05286-6

CHAPTER 3

From Dopamine Loops to Dharana: Reimagining Attention in Platform Cultures

Koteshwar Ramesh Rakesh

Abstract: The contemporary digital ecosystem is increasingly structured around platform architectures designed to capture, sustain, and monetize user attention. Social media platforms, algorithmically curated feeds, short-form video content, and AI-driven recommendation systems have contributed to the emergence of what scholars describe as the "attention economy," wherein human cognition itself becomes a commodified resource. This chapter critically examines how platform cultures cultivate compulsive engagement patterns through intermittent rewards, infinite scrolling, personalized content loops, and emotionally stimulating digital environments that contribute to cognitive overload, fragmented attention, digital fatigue, and psychological dependency. Drawing from cyberpsychology, media ecology, and communication theory, the chapter explores the psychological mechanisms underlying dopamine-driven engagement and the behavioural conditioning embedded within contemporary digital communication systems.

In response to these emerging concerns, the chapter introduces the Indic concept of *Dharana,* which is derived from classical Yogic philosophy, as an alternative framework for understanding attention, intentionality, and cognitive regulation in digitally mediated societies. Unlike platform-driven models of fragmented attention, *Dharana* emphasizes sustained concentration, mindful awareness, and disciplined engagement with stimuli. By placing Indian Knowledge Systems (IKS) in dialogue with contemporary communication and cyberpsychological discourse, this chapter proposes a culturally grounded and interdisciplinary reimagining of digital well-being and attentional resilience.

The chapter ultimately argues that integrating indigenous epistemologies into discussions of platform culture can expand existing frameworks of media literacy, digital wellness, and ethical technology design, particularly within Global South contexts. Conceptual in nature, this contribution seeks to bridge cyberpsychology, communication studies, and Indian philosophical thought to offer new directions for theorizing attention in algorithmically mediated environments.

Keywords: *Attention Economy, Platform Culture, Cyberpsychology, Digital Well-Being, Dharana, Indian Knowledge System, IKS, Algorithmic Communication*

1. Introduction

Digital technologies increasingly mediate how individuals communicate, access information, maintain relationships, and participate in public life. Social media platforms, algorithmically curated feeds, short-form video applications, and recommendation systems have become integral components of contemporary communication environments. These platforms operate within what has been described as the attention economy, where user attention functions as a valuable resource that can be captured, measured, and monetized (Simon, 1969; Zuboff, 2019). Consequently, digital engagement is no longer shaped solely by individual preferences but also by platform architectures designed to maximize visibility, interaction, and retention.

Growing concerns within cyberpsychology and communication studies suggest that these developments may have important implications for attentional functioning. Digital platforms increasingly rely on persuasive design features such as notifications, personalized recommendations, infinite scrolling, and social feedback mechanisms that encourage continuous engagement (Alter, 2018; Fogg, 2002). Although such systems enhance accessibility and connectivity, they have also raised concerns regarding distraction, cognitive overload, compulsive engagement, and difficulties sustaining attention in everyday life (Carr, 2010; Rosen et al., 2013). As digital communication becomes deeply embedded within educational, professional, and social contexts, understanding the nature of attention within platform cultures has become an important area of inquiry.

Most existing discussions of digital attention have emerged from Western psychological, behavioural, and technological perspectives. Comparatively less attention has been given to non-Western knowledge traditions that offer alternative ways of understanding cognition, self-regulation, and attentional discipline. Indian Knowledge Systems (IKS), particularly the Yogic tradition, contain extensive discussions on the regulation and cultivation of attention that remain underexplored within contemporary cyberpsychological discourse (Cornelissen et al., 2011).

One such concept is Dharana, described in Patanjali's Yoga Sutras as the deliberate stabilization of attention upon a chosen object of focus (Bryant, 2009). Unlike platform-driven models of attention characterized by continual shifts between competing stimuli, Dharana emphasizes intentionality, sustained concentration, and cognitive regulation. The concept therefore provides a useful lens through which contemporary concerns regarding attentional fragmentation may be re-examined.

This chapter places contemporary discussions of platform culture and digital attention in dialogue with Dharana as an indigenous framework of attentional regulation. Drawing from cyberpsychology, communication studies, and Indian Knowledge Systems, it proposes a Dharana-based framework for understanding attentional resilience and digital wellbeing in increasingly platformized societies.

2. Platform Culture, Attention Economy, and Attentional Fragmentation

Digital platforms have become central infrastructures through which communication, information consumption, entertainment, and social interaction are organized. Unlike earlier media systems that primarily transmitted information, contemporary platforms actively shape what users encounter, how content is prioritized, and the duration of engagement. Social networking sites, video-sharing applications, streaming services, and search engines rely heavily on algorithmic systems that personalize user experiences based on behavioural data, interaction histories, and engagement patterns (Dijck et al., 2018). As a result, communication within digital environments is increasingly influenced by computational systems designed to maximize user attention.

The economic logic underlying these systems is often described as the attention economy. Simon (1971) observed that an abundance of information inevitably creates a scarcity of attention because human cognitive resources remain limited. In contemporary digital environments, this scarcity has become economically valuable. Platform-based business models depend upon capturing and retaining user attention, transforming engagement into opportunities for data collection, behavioural prediction, and targeted advertising (Davenport & Beck, 2001; Zuboff, 2019). Attention therefore functions not only as a cognitive resource but also as a commodity within platform capitalism.

To sustain engagement, platforms frequently employ persuasive design strategies rooted in behavioural psychology. Notifications, likes, infinite scrolling, autoplay functions, and algorithmically generated recommendations encourage repeated interaction by creating cycles of anticipation and reward (Fogg, 2002). Such mechanisms often operate through variable reinforcement schedules, which have long been recognized as powerful drivers of habitual behaviour (Skinner, 1953). The rapid growth of short-form content platforms such as TikTok, Instagram Reels, and YouTube Shorts has further intensified these dynamics by providing continuous streams of personalized content with few natural stopping points (Alter, 2018).

While these systems have expanded access to information and social connectivity, they have also generated concerns regarding their impact on attentional functioning. The constant flow of notifications, updates, and competing streams of information requires individuals to allocate attention across multiple stimuli simultaneously. Under such conditions, cognitive resources become fragmented, making sustained concentration increasingly difficult (Sweller, 1988). Research on media multitasking suggests that frequent switching between digital activities is associated with greater susceptibility to distraction and reduced capacity to filter irrelevant information (Ophir et al., 2009). Similarly, repeated task switching may produce attentional residue, whereby cognitive resources remain partially engaged with previous activities even after attention has shifted elsewhere (Leroy, 2009).

Attentional fragmentation extends beyond cognitive performance and may influence emotional and behavioural functioning as well. The recurring cycles of anticipation, reward, and social validation embedded within many digital platforms can reinforce habitual checking behaviours and prolonged engagement (Montag & Walla, 2016). Over time, such patterns have been associated with cognitive overload, mental fatigue, reduced attentional control, and difficulties disengaging from digital environments (Carr, 2010; Mark et al., 2016). The resulting paradox is that technologies designed to facilitate communication and information access may simultaneously undermine the sustained attentional capacities required for reflection, learning, and deliberate engagement.

These developments suggest that attentional fragmentation should not be viewed solely as an individual failure of self-control. Rather, it emerges within communication environments deliberately structured to compete for and retain user attention. Understanding digital attention therefore requires examining both individual cognitive processes and the broader technological systems that shape them. It is within this context that alternative frameworks of attentional regulation become particularly relevant.

3. Dharana and Indian Knowledge Systems

Contemporary discussions of attention are largely informed by psychological, neuroscientific, and technological perspectives. While these approaches have generated important insights into cognitive functioning, alternative understandings of attention can also be found within non-Western knowledge traditions. Indian Knowledge Systems (IKS), particularly the Yogic tradition, contain extensive discussions on attention, self-regulation, and mental discipline that remain relatively underexplored within contemporary cyberpsychology and communication studies (Cornelissen et al., 2011).

One of the central concepts within this tradition is Dharana, described in Patanjali's Yoga Sutras as the deliberate stabilization of attention on a chosen object of focus (Bryant, 2009). Unlike ordinary states of attention, which frequently shift between external stimuli, memories, emotions, and thoughts, Dharana emphasizes sustained concentration and the intentional regulation of cognitive resources. Attention is therefore viewed not as a passive response to environmental stimuli but as a trainable capacity that can be consciously directed and maintained.

Dharana is often understood in relation to two associated concepts within the Yogic tradition: Pratyahara and Dhyana. Pratyahara refers to the regulation of attention by reducing excessive responsiveness to sensory stimulation, while Dhyana represents a more continuous and uninterrupted flow of concentration (Feuerstein, 2008). Dharana occupies an intermediate position between these states, focusing specifically on the deliberate stabilization of attention. Together, these concepts describe a progression from managing distraction to sustaining concentration.

Although rooted in a contemplative tradition, Dharana bears relevance to contemporary discussions on attentional regulation. Research on mindfulness, executive control, and attentional training has increasingly highlighted the importance of intentional attentional deployment in maintaining psychological well-being and reducing distraction (Tang et al., 2015). Dharana similarly emphasizes the capacity to direct attention voluntarily rather than allowing it to be continuously shaped by external stimuli.

This perspective becomes particularly relevant within contemporary platform cultures, where notifications, algorithmic recommendations, and personalized content streams constantly compete for cognitive resources. Whereas platform architectures often encourage rapid attentional shifts, Dharana prioritizes stability, intentionality, and sustained engagement. The concept therefore offers a useful framework for rethinking attention in digitally mediated environments and provides a foundation for exploring how attentional resilience may be cultivated within contemporary communication systems.

4. Reimagining Digital Attention Through Dharana

The growing influence of platform cultures has transformed attention from a cognitive process into an economic resource. Within contemporary digital environments, users are constantly exposed to notifications, algorithmically curated content, personalized recommendations, and social feedback mechanisms that compete for limited attentional resources. Much of the existing scholarship has examined these developments through frameworks of behavioural addiction, persuasive technology, cognitive overload, and digital wellbeing (Alter, 2018; Fogg, 2002; Zuboff, 2019). While these perspectives have contributed substantially to understanding the mechanisms through which platforms capture attention, they often remain focused on explaining the problem rather than providing alternative models of attentional engagement.

The concept of Dharana offers one such alternative. Rather than approaching attention as a scarce commodity that must be captured and retained, Dharana treats attention as a faculty that can be intentionally directed, stabilized, and regulated. This distinction represents a fundamental difference in how attention is conceptualized. Within platform cultures, attentional movement is frequently externally driven, responding to algorithmic cues, notifications, and continuously changing streams of information. Dharana, in contrast, emphasizes internally regulated attention in which the individual consciously determines the object and duration of focus (Bryant, 2009).

Table 1: Characteristics of Platformized Attention and Dharana-Based Attention

Dimension	Platformized Attention	Dharana-Based Attention
Source of attention	Algorithmic cues	Conscious intention
Pattern of engagement	Reactive	Deliberate
Temporal orientation	Rapid shifting	Sustained focus
Cognitive state	Fragmented	Integrated
Primary goal	Retention and engagement	Regulation and awareness
Psychological outcome	Overload and fatigue	Attentional resilience

The contrast presented in Table 1 highlights two fundamentally different orientations toward attention. Platform cultures operate through mechanisms designed to attract, redirect, and sustain user engagement, often encouraging rapid transitions between competing stimuli. Dharana, by comparison, emphasizes intentional attentional regulation and sustained engagement with a chosen object of focus. The distinction is not intended to portray digital technologies as inherently harmful or contemplative traditions as inherently superior. Rather, it illustrates how different systems embody different assumptions about the nature and purpose of attention. Understanding these contrasting orientations provides a foundation for examining how Dharana may function as a framework for attentional resilience within digitally mediated environments.

From this perspective, the central issue is not the existence of digital technologies themselves but the attentional habits that emerge through repeated engagement with them. Platform architectures encourage rapid shifts between stimuli, rewarding novelty, immediacy, and continuous responsiveness. Dharana encourages a different orientation toward information and communication. Attention is directed deliberately rather than reactively, engagement is governed by intention rather than impulse, and cognitive resources are allocated selectively rather than continuously dispersed across competing stimuli.

These contrasting approaches can be understood through four dimensions of digital attention: attentional orientation, attentional duration, attentional agency, and attentional outcome.

Drawing upon the preceding discussion, Figure 1 proposes a Dharana-based framework for understanding how attentional regulation may function as a compensating process within platform cultures.

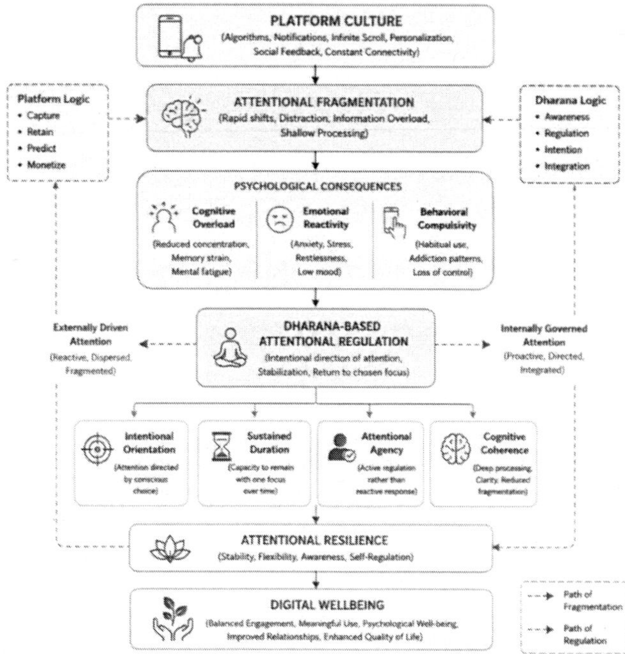

Figure 1. The Dharana Framework for Attentional Resilience in Platform Cultures (Author's own work, 2026); (Image Source: Generated using Nano Banana using a word file as context file which contained the above written text boxes and content)

The first dimension concerns *attentional orientation*. In platform environments, attention is frequently redirected by external stimuli. Notifications, recommendations, trending content, and social validation mechanisms continuously compete for cognitive resources. Under Dharana, the individual retains primary control over attentional allocation. External stimuli may still be present, but they do not determine attentional direction automatically.

The second dimension involves *attentional duration*. Contemporary digital platforms are characterized by rapid cycles of content consumption in which attention shifts repeatedly across multiple sources of information. Such conditions often encourage scanning rather than sustained engagement. Dharana places emphasis on maintaining attention over extended periods, allowing deeper cognitive processing and reflection to occur.

The third dimension concerns *agency*. Research within cyberpsychology has demonstrated that many forms of digital engagement occur automatically and habitually, often without conscious awareness of the behavioural cues triggering interaction (Montag & Walla, 2016). Dharana introduces a model in which attention becomes a matter of deliberate choice. The individual actively participates in directing cognitive resources rather than merely responding to environmental prompts.

The final dimension concerns *outcomes*. Fragmented attentional patterns may contribute to cognitive overload, digital fatigue, reduced concentration, and difficulties disengaging from digital environments (Carr, 2010). Dharana does not eliminate distraction entirely; rather, it develops the capacity to recognize distraction and repeatedly return attention to a chosen focus. The outcome is not constant concentration but greater attentional stability over time.

This framework also has implications for how digital wellbeing is conceptualized. Existing approaches frequently emphasize reducing screen time, limiting social media use, or temporarily disconnecting from digital technologies. While such strategies may be beneficial, they often frame the problem primarily in terms of exposure. A Dharana-based perspective shifts attention toward the quality of engagement rather than the quantity of usage. The question becomes not merely how much time individuals spend online but how attention is directed while engaging with digital environments.

Such a shift may be particularly relevant in contemporary societies where complete disengagement from technology is neither practical nor desirable. Educational systems, workplaces, healthcare services, and social relationships increasingly depend upon digital communication infrastructures. Under these conditions, attentional regulation may represent a more realistic objective than technological avoidance. Dharana therefore offers a framework through which digital participation and attentional discipline can coexist rather than being treated as opposing conditions.

Viewed through this lens, Dharana is not simply an ancient contemplative practice applied to a modern problem. It provides a distinct way of conceptualizing attention itself. By placing Dharana in dialogue with cyberpsychology and communication studies, attention can be understood not only as a resource targeted by platforms but also as a capacity that individuals can consciously regulate. This perspective expands current discussions on digital wellbeing by introducing a framework rooted in intentionality, attentional agency, and cognitive self-regulation.

5. Implications for Digital Wellbeing and Ethical Technology

The Dharana Framework offers a different way of approaching digital wellbeing in platformized societies. Current discussions frequently focus on reducing screen time, limiting social media use, or encouraging periodic digital detoxification. While these approaches may provide temporary relief from digital fatigue, they often treat technology itself as the primary problem. Such perspectives may overlook the fact that digital technologies have become deeply integrated into education, employment, healthcare, governance, and social relationships. Under these conditions, complete disengagement from digital environments is neither feasible nor desirable for most individuals.

A Dharana-based perspective shifts the focus from technological exposure to attentional regulation. Rather than asking how much time individuals spend online, the framework draws attention to how cognitive resources are allocated during digital engagement. Two individuals may spend similar amounts of time on digital platforms while experiencing very different psychological outcomes depending on the degree of intentionality, self-regulation, and attentional control involved in their interactions. Digital wellbeing, therefore, may be understood not only as a matter of behavioural moderation but also as a matter of attentional quality.

This perspective has implications for media literacy initiatives as well. Conventional digital literacy programmes primarily emphasize information evaluation, online safety, privacy awareness, and responsible communication. While these competencies remain important, growing concerns regarding distraction, information overload, and compulsive engagement suggest that attentional literacy may deserve equal consideration. Attentional literacy refers to the ability to recognize how digital environments influence cognitive processes and to develop skills that support intentional engagement with information. Within this context, Dharana offers a conceptual vocabulary through which attention can be understood as a trainable capacity rather than a passive response to digital stimuli.

The framework also contributes to ongoing discussions regarding ethical technology design. Contemporary platforms frequently rely on engagement-driven metrics that prioritize user retention, interaction frequency, and content consumption. Such models often reward designs that maximize attentional capture regardless of their cognitive or psychological consequences (Zuboff, 2019). Growing movements advocating humane technology have therefore called for greater consideration of user wellbeing during the design process (Harris, 2019). A Dharana-informed approach would encourage designers to consider whether digital environments support intentional engagement or merely prolong interaction.

Examples may include interface designs that create natural stopping points, reduce unnecessary interruptions, promote reflective use, and provide greater transparency regarding recommendation systems. Such approaches would not eliminate persuasive technologies altogether but would seek to balance engagement objectives with user autonomy and attentional wellbeing. Within communication studies, this raises broader questions regarding the social responsibilities of platforms that increasingly mediate public discourse, interpersonal relationships, and information consumption.

The framework may be particularly relevant within Global South contexts, where discussions of digital wellbeing have often relied upon theories developed within Western cultural settings. Indian Knowledge Systems offer conceptual resources that emerge from different assumptions regarding cognition, self-regulation, and human flourishing. Engaging with these traditions does not require rejecting contemporary psychological theories. Rather, it creates opportunities for expanding the range of perspectives available for understanding communication technologies and their effects on human behaviour. Such efforts may contribute to a more pluralistic and culturally inclusive body of scholarship within cyberpsychology and communication studies.

Future research may build upon the Dharana Framework by examining relationships between attentional regulation, digital behaviour, psychological wellbeing, and platform use across different populations. Empirical studies could explore whether practices associated with Dharana influence patterns of social media engagement, attentional control, digital fatigue, or online self-regulation. Such investigations would help clarify the extent to which concepts derived from Indian Knowledge Systems can contribute to contemporary understandings of digital life.

6. Conclusion

The rise of platform cultures has transformed attention into a valuable economic resource, giving rise to digital environments designed to maximize engagement through continuous stimulation, personalization, and behavioural reinforcement. While these systems have expanded opportunities for communication and information access, they have also contributed to growing concerns regarding attentional fragmentation, cognitive overload, and digital fatigue. This chapter argued that understanding these developments requires moving beyond conventional discussions of screen time and technology use toward a deeper examination of attentional processes themselves.

Drawing upon the concept of Dharana from Indian Knowledge Systems, the chapter proposed an alternative framework for understanding attention in digitally mediated environments. Dharana conceptualizes attention as a capacity that can be intentionally directed, stabilized, and regulated rather than passively captured by external stimuli. By placing cyberpsychology and communication studies in dialogue with Yogic understandings of concentration, the chapter offered a culturally grounded perspective on attentional resilience and digital wellbeing.

As digital technologies continue to shape everyday life, incorporating diverse intellectual traditions into discussions of attention and wellbeing may provide new directions for research, theory, and practice. Dharana offers one such perspective, inviting a reconsideration of how attention is understood, exercised, and sustained within contemporary platform societies.

References

- Alter, A. (2018). *Irresistible: The rise of addictive technology and the business of keeping us hooked*. Penguin Books.
- Bryant, E. F. (2009). *The Yoga Sūtras of Patañjali: A new edition, translation, and commentary with insights from the traditional commentators*. North Point Press.
- Carr, N. G. (2010). *The shallows: What the Internet is doing to our brains* (1st ed.). W. W. Norton.
- Cornelissen, R. M. M., Cornelissen, M., Misra, G., & Varma, S. (2011). *Foundations of Indian psychology: Volume 1, theories and concepts*. Pearson.
- Davenport, T. H., & Beck, J. C. (2001). *The attention economy: Understanding the new*

currency of business. Harvard Business School Press.

- Van Dijck, J., Poell, T., & De Waal, M. (2018). *The platform society: Public values in a connective world*. Oxford University Press. https://doi.org/10.1093/oso/9780190889760.001.0001
- Feuerstein, G. (2008). *The yoga tradition: Its history, literature, philosophy, and practice* (3rd ed.). Hohm Press.
- Fogg, B. J. (2002). Persuasive technology: Using computers to change what we think and do. *Ubiquity, 2002*(December), Article 2. https://doi.org/10.1145/764008.763957
- Harris, T. (2019, October 16). *How technology is hijacking your mind—From a former insider*. Thrive Global. https://medium.com/thrive-global/how-technology-hijacks-peoples-minds-from-a-magician-and-google-s-design-ethicist-56d62ef5edf3
- Leroy, S. (2009). Why is it so hard to do my work? The challenge of attention residue when switching between work tasks. *Organizational Behavior and Human Decision Processes, 109*(2), 168–181. https://doi.org/10.1016/j.obhdp.2009.04.002
- Mark, G., Iqbal, S. T., Czerwinski, M., Johns, P., & Sano, A. (2016). Neurotics can't focus: An in situ study of online multitasking in the workplace. In *Proceedings of the 2016 CHI*

Conference on Human Factors in Computing Systems (pp. 1739–1744). https://doi.org/10.1145/2858036.2858202

- Montag, C., & Walla, P. (2016). Carpe diem instead of losing your social mind: Beyond digital addiction and why we all suffer from digital overuse. *Cogent Psychology, 3*(1), 1157281. https://doi.org/10.1080/23311908.2016.1157281
- Ophir, E., Nass, C., & Wagner, A. D. (2009). Cognitive control in media multitaskers. *Proceedings of the National Academy of Sciences, 106*(37), 15583–15587. https://doi.org/10.1073/pnas.0903620106
- Rosen, L. D., Carrier, L. M., & Cheever, N. A. (2013). Facebook and texting made me do it: Media-induced task-switching while studying. *Computers in Human Behavior, 29*(3), 948–958. https://doi.org/10.1016/j.chb.2012.12.001
- Simon, H. A. (1969). Designing organizations for an information-rich world. In M. Greenberger (Ed.), *Computers, communication, and the public interest* (pp. 37–72). Johns Hopkins Press. https://zeus.zeit.de/2007/39/simon.pdf
- Sweller, J. (1988). Cognitive load during problem solving: Effects on learning. *Cognitive Science, 12*(2), 257–285. https://doi.org/10.1207/s15516709cog1202_4
- Tang, Y.-Y., Hölzel, B. K., & Posner, M. I. (2015). The neuroscience of mindfulness

meditation. *Nature Reviews Neuroscience, 16*(4), 213–225. https://doi.org/10.1038/nrn3916

- Zuboff, S. (2019). *The age of surveillance capitalism: The fight for a human future at the new frontier of power*. PublicAffairs.

CHAPTER 4

Redefining Media Literacy in the Age of AI: Algorithmic Literacy and Synthetic Media Resilience in India

Kaushik Roy & Dr. Chanchal Sachdeva Suri

Abstract: The rapid growth of artificial intelligence (AI)-generated content, recommender systems, and platform driven communication has significantly reshaped the contemporary information ecosystems. In India's mobile-first and multilingual digital landscape, platforms like YouTube, Instagram, Facebook, and WhatsApp are increasingly playing an important role in shaping what people see, know and engage with through algorithm driven content creation and personalized recommendations. At the same time, deepfakes, synthetic media, and AI-generated misinformation are growing and have made it increasingly difficult for users to verify sources and judge the credibility of the online content. This chapter argues that traditional media literacy approaches, that primarily focuses on critical reading and factchecking, are no longer sufficient in AI-driven communication environments. This chapter places algorithmic literacy as a much-needed extension of media literacy. Also, this chapter highlights the need for individuals to know and understand how algorithms shape content visibility, influence information exposure, and affect public penetration. Drawing on the concepts of algorithmic literacy, epistemic vigilance, and multimodal literacy - this chapter explores how AI-driven misinformation spreads across India's platform-based and vernacular digital environments. Additionally, this chapter gives due importance to short form video ecosystems, engagement-driven content systems, WhatsApp forwarding cultures, and the dissemination of misinformation in regional languages. Moreover, the chapter further argues for literacy frameworks that are context-sensitive and integrate platform awareness, the ability to discern synthetic media, and a critical understanding of how algorithm shapes and governs digital communication. By positioning India as a distinctive and underexplored context for understanding AI-led misinformation resilience, this chapter contributes to emerging discussions on media literacy, democratic engagement, and public trust in the era of AI.

Keywords: *Algorithmic Literacy, Synthetic Media, AI-generated Misinformation, Epistemic Vigilance, Multimodal Literacy, Media Literacy, India, Platform Governance*

1. Introduction

Artificial Intelligence (AI) is evolving every day. It is continuously changing today's information environments and allowing widespread creation and production of synthetic media including AI-generated text, images, audio and video content. These advancements in AI technologies have made it increasingly difficult to distinguish between real and manipulated content. The transition has created new challenges for the integrity of information, public trust and democratic communication (Westerlund, 2019; Helmus & Chandra, 2024). Meanwhile, digital platforms have become increasingly dependent on algorithmic recommendation systems. They decide what kind of information becomes visible and receives attention, how it affects users' engagement and perceptions of credibility (Kozyreva et al., 2020; Tomassi et al., 2024).

The convergence of AI-generated content and algorithmically curated information environments have heightened concerns about the spread of misinformation and disinformation. Unlike traditional forms of misinformation, AI-generated content can be created at scale, personalized for specific audiences, and amplified through automated recommendation systems, thereby increasing its reach and persuasive potential (Helmus & Chandra, 2024; Romanishyn et al., 2025). Consequently, individuals required to assess not only the credibility of information but also the technological systems that determine how information is selected, prioritized, and disseminated.

Media literacy has long been recognized as an essential tool that enables individuals to access, analyze, evaluate, and create media messages effectively (Livingstone, 2004; Buckingham, 2019). However, traditional media literacy frameworks were developed in an era when information flows were relatively transparent and human gatekeepers played an important role in content selection. In today's AI-driven media landscape, information exposure is increasingly shaped by opaque algorithms that personalize content, influence engagement, and play a significant role in shaping public understanding of social and political issues (Tomassi et al., 2024).

This transformation calls for a broader understanding of media literacy that goes beyond evaluating media content to include a knowledge of algorithmic systems and their influence on information exposure. Emerging research suggests that algorithmic literacy - the ability to recognize, understand, and critically assess algorithmic curation processes - should be viewed as an important component of contemporary media literacy frameworks (Kozyreva et al., 2020; Romanishyn et al., 2025). Despite this growing recognition, empirical and conceptual research that integrates algorithmic literacy with resilience to AI-generated misinformation remains limited, particularly in non-Western and multilingual contexts.

India offers a particularly important context for examining these challenges. As one of the world's largest digital societies, with widespread mobile-first internet access, extensive use of social media, significant linguistic diversity, and rapidly expanding AI adoption, India faces unique vulnerabilities to synthetic media and algorithmically amplified misinformation. These conditions underscore the need for context-sensitive media literacy approaches that address not only the technological factors but also the socio-cultural dimensions of consumption of information.

Accordingly, this chapter argues that algorithmic literacy should be recognized as the core component of contemporary media literacy. By exploring the intersection of AI-generated content, platform governance, and misinformation resilience, the chapter proposes a framework for enhancing citizens' capacity to critically engage with AI-mediated information environments in the Indian context.

2. Ai, Algorithms, And The Transformation Of Media Literacy

Media literacy has traditionally focused on enabling individuals to access, analyze, evaluate, and create media content. As communication technologies evolved, the concept expanded into digital literacy and information literacy, reflecting the growing need to navigate online environments and critically assess information sources (Livingstone, 2004; Buckingham, 2019). The emergence of artificial intelligence (AI) and algorithmically mediated communication has introduced a new challenge: citizens must now understand not only information itself but also the technological systems that shape how information is distributed and encountered.

Digital platforms such as YouTube, Instagram, Facebook, and WhatsApp increasingly rely on algorithmic recommendation systems to curate content. These systems use behavioral data, engagement patterns, and contextual signals to personalize information exposure, influencing what users see, share, and perceive as important (Hutchinson, 2019). Rather than acting as neutral conduits, platforms actively prioritize content that maximizes attention and engagement, creating individualized information environments that shape public understanding and opinion.

This shift has transformed information consumption from a process of active searching to one of passive recommendation. Algorithmic curation can reinforce existing preferences, increase exposure to emotionally engaging content, and contribute to selective information environments often described as filter bubbles or echo chambers (Kozyreva et al., 2020; Hutchinson, 2019). While scholars continue to debate the extent of these effects, there is broad consensus that algorithms significantly influence information visibility and public discourse.

The challenge is further intensified by the rise of generative AI and synthetic media. AI-generated text, images, audio, and video can now be produced rapidly and at scale, often appearing highly realistic and difficult to distinguish from authentic content. Deepfakes and other forms of manipulated media undermine traditional credibility cues, making it increasingly difficult for users to rely on visual or textual authenticity as indicators of truth (Westerlund, 2019; Helmus & Chandra, 2024). Moreover, algorithmic systems frequently amplify content based on engagement rather than accuracy, enabling misinformation to spread rapidly across digital networks.

These developments expose important limitations in conventional media literacy frameworks. Traditional approaches emphasize fact-checking, source verification, and critical reading skills. Although these remain essential, they do not fully address the role of algorithms in determining information exposure before users even encounter content. Understanding why particular content appears in a feed, how personalization works, and how recommendation systems shape visibility has become equally important (Kozyreva et al., 2020; Diepeveen & Pinet, 2022).

Consequently, scholars increasingly advocate for algorithmic literacy as a critical extension of media literacy. Algorithmic literacy refers to the ability to recognize, understand, and critically evaluate how algorithms influence information access, visibility, and credibility. It includes awareness of personalization mechanisms, data collection practices, recommendation systems, and platform governance structures that shape contemporary communication environments (Kozyreva et al., 2020). Rather than viewing platforms as neutral intermediaries, algorithmic literacy encourages users to understand them as active actors in the construction of knowledge and public discourse.

In the Indian context, the need for algorithmic literacy is particularly urgent. India's mobile-first digital ecosystem, widespread social media adoption, and multilingual online environment create conditions in which algorithmic systems exert substantial influence over information consumption. As AI-generated content becomes more prevalent, strengthening algorithmic literacy can help citizens better understand platform dynamics, critically evaluate digital content, and build resilience against misinformation and synthetic media. Accordingly, algorithmic literacy should be regarded as a foundational competency for media literacy in the age of AI.

3. Theoretical Framework

This chapter frames algorithmic literacy as an essential evolution of media literacy within communication spaces influenced by Artificial Intelligence. Though traditional media literacy emphasizes skills like access, analysis, evaluation, and production of content, today's digital landscapes are largely driven by automated systems deciding which information rises, spreads, or stays hidden. Because of this shift, people need awareness not just about the messages they encounter, yet also about the underlying mechanisms shaping where those messages appear - and how often (Kozyreva et al., 2020; Helmus & Chandra, 2024).

3.1 Algorithmic Literacy: Definition and Scope

Algorithmic literacy is the ability to identify, understand, and critically evaluate how algorithmic systems affect the information we are exposed to and the public discourse. It encompasses knowledge about the mechanisms of personalization, recommendation systems, platform governance and data-driven content curation that shape users' online experiences (Kozyreva et al., 2020). Algorithmic literacy lets users understand how algorithms grab attention, ensure engagement and built a perception of credibility, instead of seeing digital platforms as neutral intermediaries.

The construct is best understood as distinct from, but complementary to, existing literacy frameworks. Table 1 below shows algorithmic literacy against four neighbouring constructs, making clear its unique contribution to the literacy landscape.

Table 1: Algorithmic Literacy and Adjacent Constructs

Construct	Primary Focus	Gap Addressed by Algorithmic Literacy
Media Literacy	Evaluating media messages; source credibility	*Does not address algorithmic curation or system-level amplification logic*
Digital Literacy	Navigating digital tools and online environments	*Does not explain why specific content surfaces or how platform*

		governance works
Information Literacy	Assessing and verifying information sources	*Does not address automated ranking mechanisms or engagement-driven incentives*
AI Literacy	Understanding AI capabilities, tools, and outputs	*Does not cover platform-level recommendation decisions or curation dynamics*
Algorithmic Literacy	How automated systems shape exposure, visibility, and information credibility across platform ecosystems	— Integrative competency that addresses gaps in all the above

Table 1. Construct differentiation: Algorithmic literacy in relation to established media and digital literacy frameworks.

3.2 Epistemic Vigilance Theory

The chapter moves to the Epistemic Vigilance Theory that explains how individuals evaluate information in AI-mediated environments. The theory suggests that people evaluate information by assessing the source reliability, the message plausibility, and the consistency with existing knowledge. In AI-mediated environments, these evaluative processes become more complex because synthetic media can mimic authentic communication and exploit traditional credibility cues. Therefore, users must be more careful when evaluating information sources and claims (Germani et al., 2024; Gilbert & Gilbert, 2024).

The affective dimension of algorithmically curated content adds another layer of complexity to the difficulty of epistemic vigilance. Recommender systems systematically surface affectively charged content - outrage, fear, sensationalism that exploits affect heuristics and suppresses deliberate evaluation.

3.3 Multimodal Literacy

The framework is also informed by multimodal literacy, acknowledging that the proliferation of AI-generated misinformation increasingly blends text, image, audio, and video to produce compelling narratives. Users need to evaluate credibility across formats and check provenance while assessing various modes of communication simultaneously (Singh & Dhiman, 2023; Schipper, 2025).

3.4 The Integrated Framework: Algorithmic Literacy → Epistemic Vigilance → Synthetic Media Resilience

Algorithmic literacy, epistemic vigilance and multimodal literacy come together to create a cohesive understanding of resilience to the effects of artificial intelligence-generated misinformation. As such, algorithmic literacy provides an understanding of how information reaches the user, epistemic vigilance helps with the critical evaluation of the informativeness of information and multimodal literacy allows the user to assess different types of synthetic media via various modes.

In India, where mobile-first usage of the internet and communication in multiple languages as well as dependence on platforms shapes how one gets information, all these competencies are critical to creating informed, resilient participation in AI-mediated public discourse.

In figure 1, the integrated framework depicting this three-stage directional model is portrayed.

Figure 1: The Integrated Three-Stage Literacy Framework

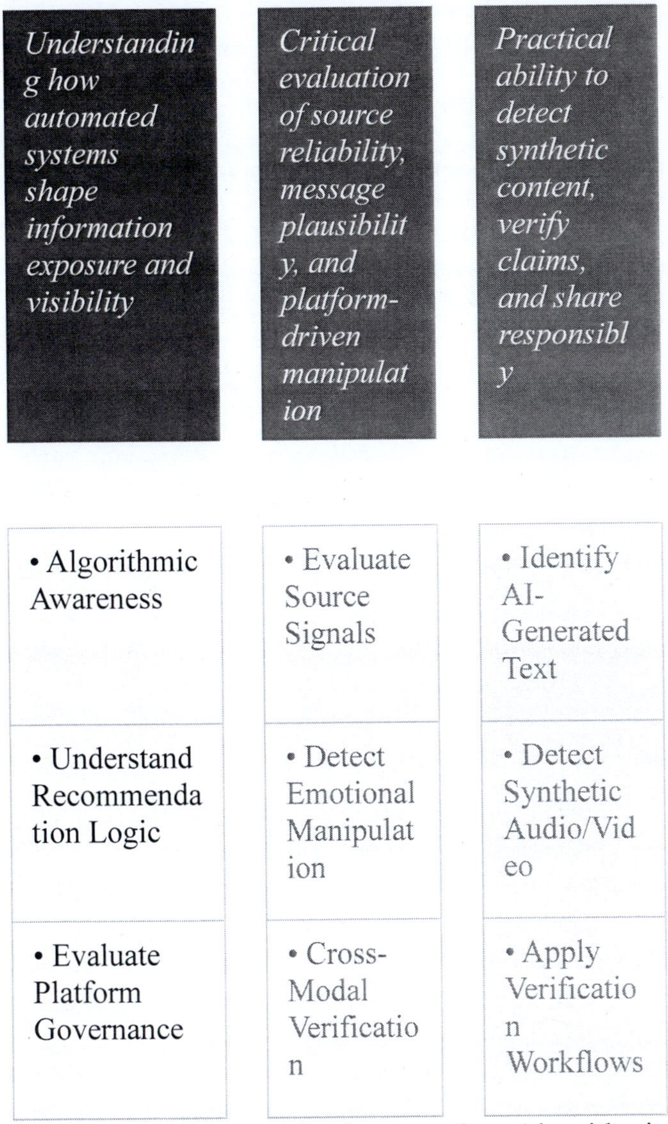

Figure 1. Integrated framework: Algorithmic Literacy enables Epistemic Vigilance, together

producing Synthetic Media Resilience. Sub-skills for each stage are listed in the lower rows.

4. Why Algorithmic Literacy Matters In India

India provides one of the world's most significant contexts for understanding how the algorithmic systems, synthetic media, and media literacy interact together. As per IAMAI the Internet and Mobile Association of India, in 2024 India had 886 million (approx.) active internet users. Their projections indicating that the number will cross 900 million in 2025, making India one of the largest digital populations globally. India has also advanced into a mobile-first digital ecosystem with smartphones. Smartphone today has become the primary tool of accessing internet for most users. As a result, instead of traditional media - social media platforms, search engines, recommendation systems, and messaging applications have become core to how people get information, engage in public discussions and make sense of current events.

India's information environment is also characterized by great linguistic and cultural diversity. Internet access has grown rapidly, largely driven by users consuming content in regional and vernacular languages, creating complex communication networks across multiple linguistic communities. This has made digital participation larger, but also created problems for content moderation and information verification. Studies show that the spread of misinformation is driven by culturally appealing narratives and localized communication networks, which makes corrective interventions especially challenging (Badrinathan & Chauchard, 2024). These concerns are compounded by the rise of generative AI, which can create synthetic text, images, audio and video customized for particular linguistic and cultural groups.

In India's digital communication ecosystem, the Messaging platforms play a very important role. As per The Reuters Digital News Report, WhatsApp is one of the most commonly used platforms for news sharing and exchange of information among Indian users. In India's digital communications landscape, messaging services occupy a vital role within that framework. According to the Reuters Digital News Report, WhatsApp ranks among one of the most popular mediums for sharing news and disseminating information across Indian users. Since the majority of information shared via trusted personal relationships (e.g., families, communities, friendships) allows for rapid dissemination of misinformation; conventional fact-checking mechanisms may encounter difficulties in combating this type of information spread (Badrinathan & Chauchard, 2023).

Hence, Algorithmic Literacy is critical as access to information is increasingly shaped by recommendation systems designed to maximize user engagement instead of priritizing informational quality. Short-form video platforms, algorithmically curated social media feeds, and AI-powered recommendation engines play an important role in what users see, what they share, and what they perceive as trustworthy. Without an understanding of how these systems work, individuals may be more susceptible to the effects of personalization, algorithmic amplification, and engagement-driven distortions of information exposure.

Research on misinformation interventions in India shows that context-specific literacy programs can improve critical evaluation skills and reduce susceptibility to misleading information (Harjani et al., 2023). However, most of these initiatives focus on factchecking and content verification instead of understanding the algorithmic systems that shape information visibility and exposure.

Recent developments highlight these vulnerabilities. During India's 2024 general elections, AI-generated political content, including deepfakes and synthetic audio were circulated widely across social media and messaging platforms. Such incidents demonstrate how generative AI can amplify misinformation risks within India's multilingual and platform-dependent digital ecosystem.

Figure 2 outlines the key features of India's information ecosystem and their implications for algorithmic literacy.

INDIA'S AI-MEDIATED INFORMATION ECOSYSTEM AND ALGORITHMIC LITERACY IMPERATIVES		
SCALE & DIVERSITY	PLATFORM ECOSYSTEM	MISINFORMATION VULNERABILITIES
886M+ active internet users (IAMAI, 2024)	WhatsApp — primary news & information channel	AI-generated political content (2024 elections)
Projected 900M+ users by 2025	YouTube — algorithmically curated video content	Vernacular deepfakes tailored to linguistic communities
Predominantly mobile-first access	Instagram / Facebook — social news feeds	Forwarding chains bypassing fact-checking networks

22+ scheduled languages; 100s of dialects	ShareChat / Moj / Josh — vernacular short-video	Encrypted messaging limits moderation capacity
Digital divide across urban–rural & education lines	Telegram — political broadcast channels	Engagement algorithms amplifying sensational content

Key Insight: India's unique combination of scale, linguistic diversity, and platform dependency creates both heightened exposure to AI-generated misinformation and a significant opportunity to develop context-sensitive algorithmic literacy frameworks applicable to multilingual Global South contexts.

Figure 2. India's AI-mediated information ecosystem: Scale, platform landscape, and misinformation vulnerabilities driving the need for algorithmic literacy.

Consequently, algorithmic literacy should be recognized as a foundational civic competency in contemporary India. Media literacy frameworks must extend beyond fact-checking to include an understanding of recommendation systems, platform governance, personalization, and AI-generated content. Such an approach can strengthen citizen's ability to navigate and critically evaluate information in increasingly AI-mediated information environments.

5. Discussion And Implications

The following discussion shows that traditional models of media literacy are notenough to address the barriers connected with AI-made misinformation. While things like verification of source, checking fact, and critical consumption remain important, they are often less effective in digital environments where algorithms influence information exposure and synthetic media can closely mimic authentic content. Due to these evolving conditions, this changing landscape advocates a broader literacy framework that integrates media literacy, AI literacy, and algorithmic literacy.

The main conclusion of the chapter is the need to consider algorithmic literacy as an independent and measurable skill in the modern media literacy education process. Citizens must understand how information is created and how recommendation systems, personalization mechanisms and platform governance structures shape what information becomes visible and credible. This kind of awareness can help users critically interpret their digital surroundings, rather than passively consuming algorithmically curated content.

The framework proposed in this chapter also emphasizes the need for synthetic media resilience development. Resilience should not only be the ability to detect deepfakes or AI-generated content. Instead, it requires more general competencies such as questioning the sources of information, understanding the incentives of platforms, assessing multimodal content, and recognizing how emotional involvement can affect the sharing of information. These skills are becoming increasingly important as generative AI technologies continue to evolve and become more accessible.

The implications are far-reaching in Indian context. The multilingual communication environment in India and the prevalence of social media platforms and mobile internet provide a conducive environment for the fast spread of misinformation across communities. As such, media literacy interventions need to be adapted to local contexts rather than simply imported from models developed in Western contexts. Educational efforts should incorporate vernacular languages, culturally relevant examples and platform-specific learning experiences that reflect the way Indians actually access and share information online.

The chapter also has implications for policy makers, educators and platform providers. Schools and universities can integrate algorithmic literacy into their digital literacy programs, and governments and civil society organizations can conduct public awareness campaigns about misinformation produced by AI. Along with this, technology platforms should be more transparent about recommendation systems, content moderation practices and disclosures on AI-generated content.

Building resilience to misinformation is a shared responsibility that includes individual skills and institutional accountability. Ultimately, algorithmic literacy should be seen as a democratic need, not just a technical skill. As information environments are increasingly mediated by artificial intelligence, citizens need to understand, question and critically engage with the systems that shape public knowledge. The development of these competencies may contribute to a more informed, resilient and participatory digital society.

6. Conclusion

The conditions of information production, dissemination, and consumption are being fundamentally changed by the Generative AI, synthetic media, and algorithmically curated communication environments. Traditional media literacy frameworks still have an importance, but they are no longer enough to address the barriers created by AI-generated misinformation.

This chapter has argued that algorithmic literacy should be recognised as a core component of contemporary media literacy., Building on perspectives from algorithmic literacy, epistemic vigilance, and multimodal literacy - this chapter provides a framework for strengthening individuals' resilience towards synthetic media and AI-driven misinformation. Such resilience extends beyond the ability to assess the credibility of content. This resilience requires an understanding of the algorithmic systems that shape information visibility, influence public attention, and determine which voices get attention in the digital environments.

The Indian context focuses on the urgency of this challenge. As a nation with world's largest digital societies, India is characterised by mobile-first internet access, significant linguistic diversity and an increasing dependence on digital platforms for information and communication. These conditions result in the creation of an information environment with complexity – an environment in which algorithmic systems play an increasingly important role in shaping public discourse and exposure of information. Strengthening algorithmic literacy within such a context can give support to more informed decision-making while increasing resilience to misinformation and encouraging responsible participation in an increasingly digital and AI-mediated landscape.

As AI technologies continue to evolve, future media literacy initiatives must move focus beyond content-focused strategies and get a broader grasp on the socio-technical systems that shape how information flows. Algorithmic literacy offers a valuable way to equip citizens with the knowledge and critical skills required to navigate the complexities of AI mediated communication in India and beyond.

References

- Badrinathan, S., & Chauchard, S. (2023). "I don't think that's true, bro!" Social corrections of misinformation in India. *The International*

Journal of Press/Politics, 29(2), 394–416. https://doi.org/10.1177/19401612231158770

➢ Badrinathan, S., & Chauchard, S. (2024). Researching and countering misinformation in the Global South. *Current Opinion in Psychology, 55*, 101733. https://doi.org/10.1016/j.copsyc.2023.101733

➢ Buckingham, D. (2019). Teaching media in a "post-truth" age: Fake news, media bias and the challenge for media/digital literacy education. *Culture and Education, 31*(2), 213–231. https://doi.org/10.1080/11356405.2019.1603814

➢ Diepeveen, S., & Pinet, M. (2022). User perspectives on digital literacy as a response to misinformation. *Development Policy Review, 40*(S2), e12671. https://doi.org/10.1111/dpr.12671

➢ Germani, F., Spitale, G., & Biller-Andorno, N. (2024). The dual nature of AI in information dissemination: Ethical considerations. *JMIR AI, 3*, e53505. https://doi.org/10.2196/53505

➢ Gilbert, C., & Gilbert, M. A. (2024). Leveraging artificial intelligence (AI) as a strategic defense against deepfakes and digital misinformation. *International Journal of Scientific Research and Modern Technology, 3*(11), 62–78. https://doi.org/10.38124/ijsrmt.v3i11.76

➢ Harjani, T., Basol, M.-S., Roozenbeek, J., & van der Linden, S. (2023). Gamified inoculation against misinformation in India: A randomized control trial. *Journal of Trial and Error, 3*(1), 14–56. https://doi.org/10.36850/e12

- Helmus, T. C., & Chandra, B. S. S. (2024). *Generative artificial intelligence threats to information integrity and potential policy responses*. RAND Corporation. https://doi.org/10.7249/PEA3089-1

- Hutchinson, J. (2019). Digital first personality: Automation and influence within evolving media ecologies. *Convergence, 26*(5–6), 1284–1300. https://doi.org/10.1177/1354856519858921

- Internet and Mobile Association of India (IAMAI), & Kantar. (2024). *Internet in India report 2024*. IAMAI. https://www.iamai.in/sites/default/files/research/Kantar_%20IAMAI%20report_2024_.pdf

- Kozyreva, A., Lewandowsky, S., & Hertwig, R. (2020). Citizens versus the internet: Confronting digital challenges with cognitive tools. *Psychological Science in the Public Interest, 21*(3), 103–156. https://doi.org/10.1177/1529100620946707

- Livingstone, S. (2004). Media literacy and the challenge of new information and communication technologies. *The Communication Review, 7*(1), 3–14. https://doi.org/10.1080/10714420490280152

- Reuters Institute for the Study of Journalism. (2024). *Digital news report 2024*. University of Oxford.

https://reutersinstitute.politics.ox.ac.uk/digital-news-report/2024

- Romanishyn, A., Malytska, O., & Goncharuk, V. A. (2025). AI-driven disinformation: Policy recommendations for democratic resilience. *Frontiers in Artificial Intelligence, 8*, Article 1569115. https://doi.org/10.3389/frai.2025.1569115

- Schipper, T. (2025). Disinformation by design: Leveraging solutions to combat misinformation in the Philippines' 2025 election. *Data & Policy, 7*, e18. https://doi.org/10.1017/dap.2025.18

- Singh, P., & Dhiman, B. (2023). Exploding AI-generated deepfakes and misinformation: A threat of global concern in the 21st century. *TechRxiv*. https://doi.org/10.36227/techrxiv.24715605.v1

- Tomassi, A., Falegnami, A., & Romano, E. (2024). Mapping automatic social media information disorder: The role of bots and AI in spreading misleading information in society. *PLOS ONE, 19*(5), e0303183. https://doi.org/10.1371/journal.pone.0303183

- Westerlund, M. (2019). The emergence of deepfake technology: A review. *Technology Innovation Management Review, 9*(11), 39–52. https://doi.org/10.22215/timreview/1282

CHAPTER 5

Revisiting 'Meena' in the Digital Age: Sustainability Communication & SDG Recal

Dr. Shatabdi Som & Sourav Manna

Abstract: Digital media has transformed the way we communicate about sustainability, creating new avenues to reach young audiences with narratives on development. This paper investigates the effectiveness of UNICEF's Meena Communication Initiative (MCI) in enhancing students' recall of Sustainable Development Goals (SDGs). The study draws on Bandura's Social Learning Theory, Jenkins' Participatory Culture Theory, and the Elaboration Likelihood Model to explore the effect of exposure, storytelling, visual appeal, and emotional appeal on SDG recall and sustainable behavioural intentions. Data were collected using a descriptive quantitative design from 222 college going students in Kolkata, India, after watching selected Meena episodes on digital platforms. Results indicate that sustainability communication exposure substantially improves SDG recall and storytelling is the most powerful predictor of message retention. Visual appeal increases memorability and emotional appeal has a positive effect on sustainable behavioural intentions. The study highlights the sustained relevance of Meena as an entertainment-education tool, and demonstrates the potential of digital narratives to promote sustainability awareness, SDG understanding, and behavioural engagement among students.

Key words: *Sustainability Communication, SDG Recall, Meena Communication Initiative, Digital Media, Storytelling*

1. Introduction:

A nine-year-old girl of South Asian descent became the mascot of social change in every Indian household as well as Asian countries. Her mundane world resonated with uncountable children watching her fighting battles for equity. Her stories revolved around her village, family, school, friends, her brother Raju and the pet parrot Mitthu (her alter ego). For decades Meena has been the icon for health, education, gender equality, and child rights; developed by UNICEF, Meena gained popularity in South Asia as an advocacy and instructional tool for a range of social and child related issues in South Asian Countries. To develop targeted and effective health communication strategies, it is crucial to examine how communities engage in discussions and exchange information on health issues across online platforms. Such insights enable interventions to be tailored to distinct audience segments and their communication patterns (Lutkenhaus, 2020).

The proliferation of digital media has transformed the landscape of communication for development. Social media platforms, over the top platforms, video-sharing websites, and online entertainment educational resources have emerged as omnipotent tools for engaging young audiences with messages related to sustainability. Social media is crucial in influencing people's understanding of sustainability: YouTube is a major source of instructional information, Facebook encourages community involvement, and Instagram promotes aspirational consumption (Horrich, et al., 2025). In order to accomplish the general objectives of sustainable development and societal transformation, development communication and social change are dialogue based social processes that use a variety of instruments and techniques. (Ihsaniyati, et al., 2023). *Meena*, a communication initiative created by UNICEF in the 1990s, is one of the most significant examples of entertainment education in South Asia. Meena Communication Initiative (MCI) addressed important topics such as girls' education, child rights, health, sanitation, gender equality, domestic violence, immunization and social inclusion via animated stories, comics, radio shows, and instructional materials.

The Meena episodes were originally created for conventional media platforms (DD National), the narratives are still having significant visibility on digital channels, especially YouTube, introducing Meena and her world to a new range of audience. In the foreword of 'Meeting Meena' (2001), a documentation study on utilisation of Meena Communication Initiative, Nigel Fisher (Regional Director, UNICEF, South Asia, 2001) mentions that as a symbol of girl child and an advocate of children's rights, Meena has made her voice heard with her enduring popular appeal. According to social cognition theory and research, social models greatly speed up and ease the learning process (Bandura & McDonald, 1963; Van, 2004).

Meena Communication Initiative (MCI) places strong emphasis on formative research, viewing participants not merely as a target audience but as active collaborators in content creation. Once a social issue is identified, researchers engage directly with communities to understand their experiences, perceptions, and locally relevant solutions, ensuring that the resulting media content is both credible and contextually grounded ('Meeting Meena', Documentation Study, 2001). Through encouraging involvement, knowledge exchange, empowerment, and group action, communication acts as a catalyst for social change (Servaes, 2020).

Cartoon girl champions equality

Figure 1: Coverage of 'Meena' in The Times of London, 2020

Figure 2: Meena Poster by UNICEF, India

A Meena stamp was developed in collaboration with the Government

Figure 3: Postal Stamp featuring Meena

Figure 4: Snippet of Meena, Raju & Mithu

Source: Meeting Meena: Documentation study on utilisation of Meena Communication Initiative, UNICEF (ROSA)

1.1 The Meena Communication Initiative (MCI): Origin and Impact

Individuals' belief system, knowledge and attitude can be shaped through persuasive and compelling narratives (Green & Brock, 2000) and narrative theories provide a room to create storylines blending entertainment and education. The Meena communication Initiative (MCI) includes episodes of stories crafted in animation, for television, radio, comic books and other media promoting child rights and support implementation with special focus on the girl child. The campaign focussed to improve their status and develop the potential of the girl child by supporting social & behavioural change in the region.

Meena comics are a potent message that combines engaging and interactive education with the ability to change behaviors and attitudes that hinder children's development, safety, and survival. A plethora of research studies conducted for more than a decade by UNICEF and other organizations had recorded multiple facets and levels of discrimination against girls in the region (Aghi & Carnegie, 1996).The democratization of the digital sources of information, decades old UNICEF's 'Meena' initiative has carved space through transmedia storytelling and support recall the Sustainable Development Goals.

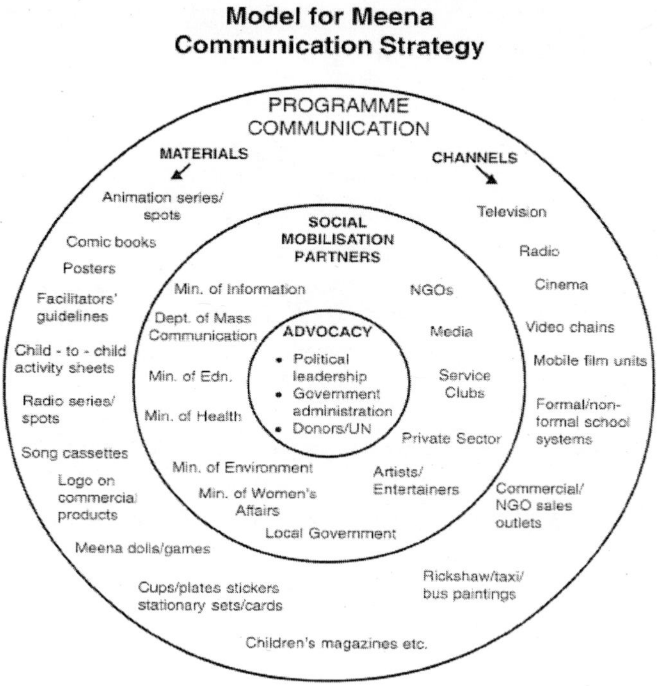

Figure 5: Model for Meena Communication Strategy, Source: UNICEF

The statement of the goal and objectives of MCI, as given in the 1999 project documents, are as follows: ('Meeting Meena', Documentation Study, 2001, UNICEF). The overall goal statement comprised the framework of the Convention on the Rights of the Child, to promote the status and development of children in South Asia, with a special focus on girls.

General Objectives

i. to research, develop and disseminate a multi-media communication package, adaptable to the needs of participating countries, to support advocacy, social mobilisation and programme communication on the issues of child rights in South Asia.

ii. to influence and support the forces of social and behavioural change concerning the Girl Child at national, community and family levels.

iii. to promote Meena as a dynamic role model for children, especially girls, through which they can acquire self-esteem and learn life-skills essential for their empowerment.

iv. to empower families, including children, with information related to the survival and development of children, including specific messages on their health, nutrition and education.

Meena's presence in South Asian popular culture is notable, relatable and prime in disseminating developmental messages. Characters, societal issues and storylines are crafted in a way that have been adapted into sustainability education, school curricula, community theater, and public health campaigns, suggesting deep cultural relevance (Chatterjee et al., 2018). The contemporary relevance of *Meena* lies in its alignment with several SDGs, including Quality Education (SDG 4), Gender Equality (SDG 5), Good Health and Well-being (SDG 3), Reduced Inequalities (SDG 10), and Clean Water and Sanitation (SDG 6). The stories of *Meena* episodes promote values and behaviours that contribute to sustainable development promoting behaviour change among the viewers. However, despite the widespread availability of digital content, limited research has examined whether students are able to recall and connect these messages with broader sustainability goals in the digital era.

The vivid animated imagery and lucid narratives on attitudinal shifts toward gender equity, with increased support for girls' education (Chesterton, 2004), challenging stereotypical gender roles, equal food distribution among boys and girls promoting sustainable food and nutrition. In the episode of *'Say No to Dowry'* Meena and her family take steps to fight against the practice of dowry. In *'Too Young to Marry'*, MCI communicates the issue of girl child's marriage in south Asian countries. The role of a mentor and school in child development is emphasised in the episode of *'I Love School'*. The communication initiative fights the stigma and shatters myths surrounding AIDS in *'AIDS: A Girl's Story'*.

This study revisits *Meena* as a development communication tool and investigates its effectiveness in fostering sustainability awareness and SDG recall among students. By examining students' exposure to selected *Meena* videos on digital platforms and assessing their understanding of sustainability-related themes, the study seeks to explore the continuing relevance of entertainment-educational media narratives in promoting sustainable development.

1.2 Entertainment-Education: Theoretical Foundations and Evolution

Entertainment education involves an effective phenomenon using the appeal of any popular media on television or radio to reach the desired group of target audience to introduce new norms and knowledge (Bouman, 1999, 2016; Chatterjee et al., 2017; Singhal & Rogers, 2004). Audience attitudes and behavioural intentions are shaped via observational learning through modeled behaviour, especially when characters are relatable and rewarded (Bandura, 2001). Meena was specifically created to serve as a role model for teenage females in the area as a young South Asian girl negotiating gender conventions, education, and health. Effective storytelling is more of an art than a formula, whether it is presented in writing, on the radio, or on television (Green & Brock, 2005). Entertainment-education strategies that combine storytelling with developmental messages have gained popularity in the digital media platforms.

The studies on '*Akili and M*e' discuss the use of music and colour, characters, making children familiar thus enhancing cognition, retention, recall of information (McCorry & Maniatopoulos, 2026). These methods make difficult societal concerns approachable and remembered by using familiar stories and relatable characters. During health emergencies, brief, animated, wordless movies disseminated by health authorities on social media might be a useful means of quick global health communication (Vandormae, et al. 2021). In Sub-

Saharan Africa, an animated children's educational programme called 'Akili and Me' offers lessons that are suited for the children's age and are culturally relatable. This study adds to the body of knowledge on instructional media by demonstrating how preschoolers who are at risk may learn socio-emotional and health-related lessons via an animated programme (Kauffman, Dura & Borzekowsk, 2022). For adolescent audiences, parasocial relationships with animated characters can be as influential as those with live-action figures, particularly when characters share demographic and situational similarities with viewers (Hoffner & Buchanan, 2005). Meena, her family, friends and community are familiar and share similar situations relevant to Indian context. The migration of Entertainment-Education content to digital platforms introduces both opportunities and complications. Transmedia storytelling extending narratives across television, apps, social media can deepen engagement (Jenkins, 2006), but also fragments attention and complicates message consistency (Scolari, 2009).

1.3 : Research Gap

Despite extensive research on entertainment-education, development communication and sustainability awareness, little research has been done on the relevance of UNICEF's Meena in the digital era. Most of the existing literature has studied Meena in the context of child rights, health and gender equality. The research on sustainability communication has mostly been done on social media campaigns and environmental advocacy.

Moreover, little research has been conducted into the effects of storytelling, visual attractiveness and emotional involvement in digitized entertainment-education content on students' SDG recall, behavioural intention and engagement in sustainability-related activities. This study fills this gap by examining the effectiveness of Meena's digital narratives in creating sustainability awareness and SDG recall among college going students in Kolkata.

1.3 : Objectives of the study

1. To examine the relationship between exposure to sustainability-driven media content and SDG recall among students.
2. To assess the influence of visual elements, storytelling-based sustainability communication and emotional appeals on students' recall of Sustainable Development Goals (SDGs) and sustainable behavioural intentions.
3. To determine whether greater exposure to sustainability communication encourages students' participation in sustainability-related activities.

1.4: Conceptual Framework

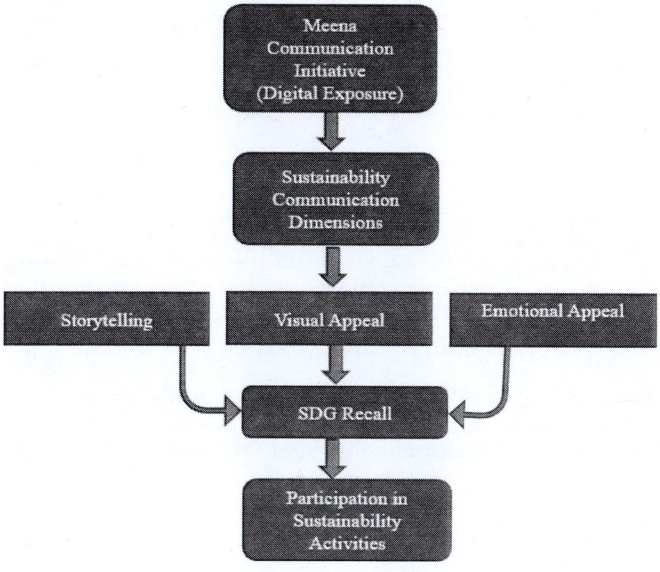

Figure 6: Conceptual Framework of the Study

The conceptual framework illustrates how digital exposure to the Meena Communication Initiative promotes sustainability communication among students. Through storytelling, visual appeal, and emotional appeal, the initiative enhances SDG recall and understanding of sustainability issues. Increased SDG recall subsequently encourages greater participation in sustainability-related activities.

1.5: Hypotheses

The following hypotheses are formulated to understand the relationship between the independent and dependent variables.

H1: Exposure to sustainability-driven media content is positively associated with SDG recall.

H2: Storytelling-based sustainability communication significantly improves SDG recall among students.

H3: Visual elements in sustainability campaigns positively influence message memorability.

H4: Emotional appeals in sustainability campaigns positively influence sustainable behavioural intentions.

H5: Students with higher exposure to sustainability communication demonstrate greater participation in sustainability-related activities.

2. Methodology

2.1 Research Design

The study adopted a descriptive quantitative approach to study the relationship between exposure to sustainability communication through the episodes of Meena Communication initiative (MCI) and the students' level of awareness, recall and practice of sustainable development goals. The population of the study consisted of students studying at UG level in educational institutions of Kolkata, West Bengal. A total of 222 respondents participated in the study and sample was selected using purposive sampling considering respondents with exposure to digital media, access to YouTube and willingness to participate in the study.

The children were shown selected episodes of 'Meena' (*Count Your Chickens, Dividing the Mango, Saving a Life, Say No to Dowry, Will Meena Leave School?)* prior to data collection. A structured questionnaire consisting of close-ended questions measured on a five-point Likert scale ranging from Strongly Disagree (1) to Strongly Agree (5). The sample consisted of 135 females (60.8%) and 87 males (39.2%) of 15-25 years and mainly consisted of undergraduate students from higher education institutions. Inclusion criteria were access to digital media, familiarity with YouTube, exposure to the selected Meena episodes and willingness to participate in the study. The study excluded those who did not consent, could not access the digital media platforms and did not fill out the questionnaire.

2.2. Defining variables

Communicating sustainability is the dissemination of messages related to sustainability through the episodes of Meena which covers themes of health, education, gender equality and social development (Servaes, 2020; Ihsaniyati et al., 2023). Sustainability awareness is the knowledge students have about sustainability issues and their importance for society. SDG recall refers to how well the respondents recall and identify the sustainability themes and Sustainable Development Goals presented in the videos. Behavioural intention is defined as the readiness to adopt sustainable practices after exposure to the contents, and participation is the actual or intended involvement in sustainability related activities and initiatives (Bandura, 2001; Singhal & Rogers, 2002; Petty & Cacioppo, 1986). These constructs of exposure, recall, attitudes, intentions, and participation were measured with Likert-scale items.

2.3. Theoretical Background

The study is grounded on Bandura's *Social Learning Theory*, Jenkins *Participatory Culture Theory* and Petty & Cacioppo's *Elaboration Likelihood Model*. The Social Learning Theory claims that individuals learn values, attitudes, behaviours through observation as well as imitations of role models. In this study 'Meena' serves as a role model demonstrating the values related to education, health, gender equity, inclusivity and sustainability. This theory is predicated on the notion that we pick up knowledge via social interactions with other people. Individually, people pick up similar tendencies by seeing how others behave (Nabavi & Bijandi, 2012).

The study also considered Jenkins Participatory Culture Theory that argues that digital media has transformed passive consumers to active participants who discuss, create, share and circulate the media content. Through YouTube the students engage with Meena Communication Initiative fostering a stronger retention and recall of sustainability driven messages. The effects of participatory culture on education and media literacy are examined in the chapter "Learning and Literacy" (Henry Jenkins' book, *Mimi Ito, and Danah Boyd, Participatory Culture in a Networked Era*). In order to characterize the learning activities carried out by the currently networked participants, the authors have applied a broader definition of literacy, characterizing literacy as the ability to engage in a larger social system rather than just the ability to create and consume information (Wang, 2018).

The Elaboration Likelihood Model emphasises on the dual pathways of persuasion: the *central route*, characterised by meticulous analysis of content, and the *peripheral route*, relying on the superficial indicators like emotional appeal. Emotional appeals often activate the *peripheral pathway*, provoking fast, immensely gratifying but momentary reactions, while logical appeals stimulate the *central route,* resulting in persistent analysis as opined by Petty & Cacioppo (1986).

2.4: Informed consent

All participants were informed about the purpose of the study and their voluntary participation. Informed consent was obtained from all individual participants included in the study before data collection. The study was approved by the concerned academic authority for ethics, ensuring that it adhered to the research ethics guidelines. The confidentiality and anonymity of the participants were strictly observed and all the responses were used for academic and research purposes only.

3. Analysis & Discussion: Watching Meena in the Digitised Platforms, Recall of SDGs and Behaviour Change

The findings of the study can be effectively interpreted through the combined lens of Bandura's Social Learning Theory and Jenkins' Participatory Culture Theory. Bandura (1977) argues that individuals acquire knowledge, attitudes, and behaviours through observation, imitation, and reinforcement. In the context of sustainability communication, students exposed to sustainability-oriented media content learn by observing the actions, consequences, and values portrayed through media narratives. The reliability analysis revealed high internal consistency for the constructs. Storytelling exhibited a Cronbach's alpha of 0.869, while Behaviour Change showed an alpha of 0.863, indicating excellent reliability of the scales.

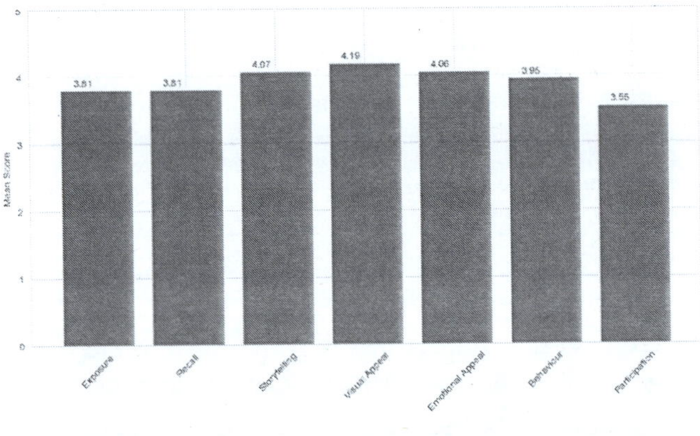

Figure 7: Mean score of study constructs

Figure 7 illustrates the average scores of the study constructs as the visual appeal received the highest mean score (4.19), followed by storytelling (4.07) and emotional appeal (4.06). Participation in sustainability-related activities recorded the lowest mean score (3.55), suggesting that although respondents demonstrate favourable attitudes toward sustainability communication, translating these attitudes into actual participation remains relatively challenging.

3.1 Exposure to Sustainability Communication Positively Influences SDG Recall

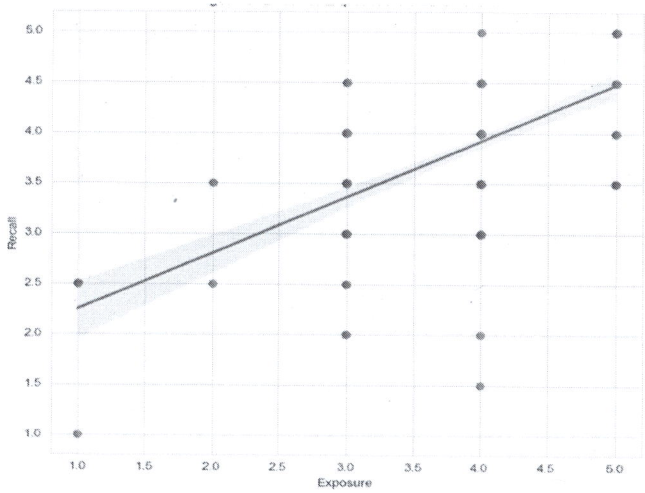

Figure 8 : Effect of Exposure on SDG Recall

The findings revealed that exposure to sustainability-driven media content significantly predicted SDG recall among students ($\beta = 0.558$, $p < 0.001$), explaining 38.3% of the variance in recall ($R^2 = 0.383$). This suggests that repeated exposure to sustainability messages through digital media enhances students' ability to remember Sustainable Development Goals. The finding supports Bandura's Social Learning Theory, which posits that learning occurs through observation and repeated exposure to modeled information. Students who frequently encounter sustainability narratives are more likely to internalize and retain sustainability-related concepts.

3.2: Storytelling-Based Communication Positively Influences SDG Recall

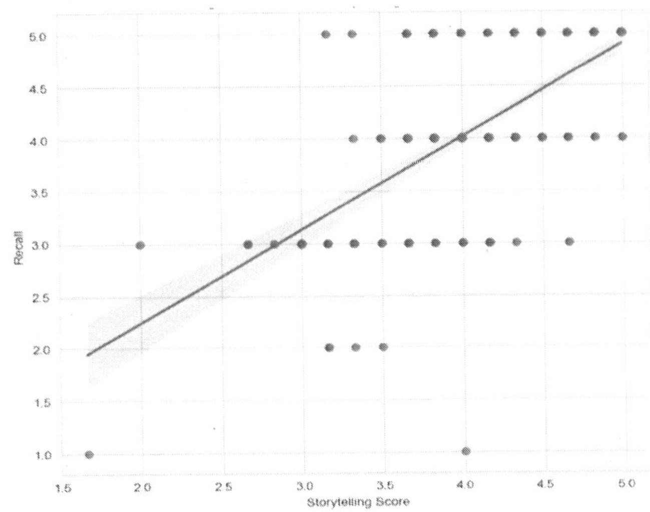

Figure 9: Effect of storytelling on SDG Recall

Storytelling emerged as the strongest predictor of SDG recall ($\beta = 0.885$, $p < 0.001$), accounting for 44.8% of the variance in recall ($R^2 = 0.448$). This finding indicates that narratives significantly enhance students' ability to remember sustainability messages. Stories provide context, emotional connection, and cognitive structure, making complex concepts easier to understand and recall. The result supports Jenkins' Participatory Culture Theory, which argues that meaningful engagement with media content increases learning outcomes. The finding also aligns with communication research suggesting that narrative transportation improves message retention and knowledge recall. In the context of Meena, storytelling enables students to relate sustainability issues to everyday experiences, thereby strengthening SDG recall.

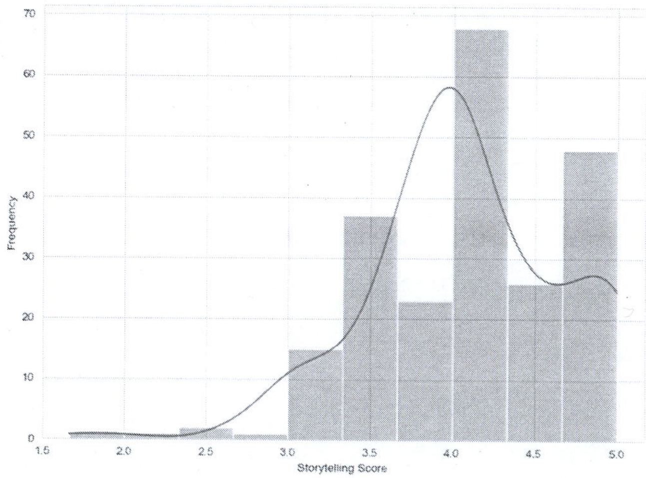

Figure 10: Distribution of Storytelling Scores

It presents the distribution of storytelling scores. Most respondents assigned relatively high scores, indicating favourable perceptions regarding the effectiveness of storytelling in sustainability communication.

3.3: Visual elements in sustainability campaigns positively influence message memorability

The results indicate that visual appeal significantly influences SDG recall among students ($\beta = 0.513$, $p < 0.001$). Visual elements such as images, animations, infographics, and videos enhance the memorability of sustainability messages by attracting attention and simplifying complex information. The model explains 22.5% of the variance in SDG recall ($R^2 = 0.225$), suggesting that visual communication plays an important role in reinforcing learning outcomes. However, its explanatory power is lower than that of storytelling, indicating that visuals alone are insufficient for maximizing recall. Thus, visual appeal supports message retention but is most effective when integrated with compelling narratives.

3.4: Emotional Appeal Positively Influences Sustainable Behavioural Intentions

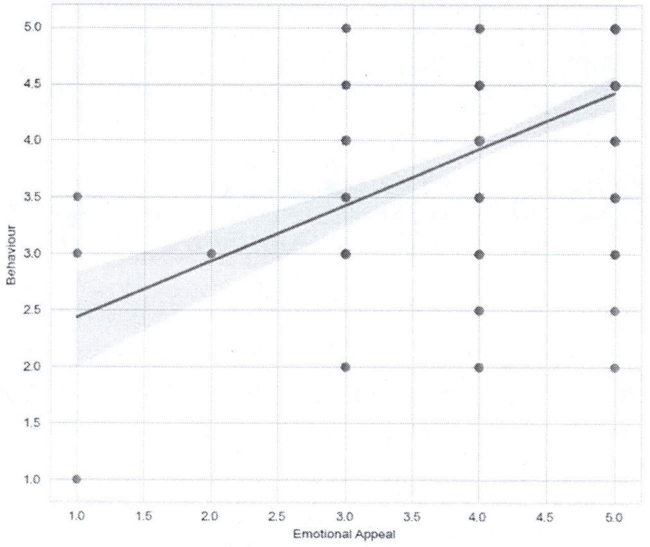

Figure 11: Effect of Emotional Appeal on Behavioral Intentions

The results demonstrated a significant positive relationship between emotional appeal and behavioural intentions (β = 0.497, $p < 0.001$), explaining 26.9% of the variance in behavioural intentions ($R^2 = 0.269$). Emotional content appears to motivate students to consider adopting sustainable behaviours by creating empathy and personal relevance. Campaigns that portray environmental challenges, social inequalities, or future consequences are more likely to evoke emotional responses that encourage behavioural change. This finding aligns with persuasive communication theories, which suggest that emotions play a crucial role in influencing attitudes and behavioural intentions. The result indicates that sustainability communication should move beyond factual information and incorporate emotional narratives to encourage action. The findings supporting H4 can be interpreted through the Elaboration Likelihood Model (ELM) proposed by Petty and Cacioppo (1986). ELM suggests that persuasion occurs through two routes: the central route, involving careful evaluation of message content, and the peripheral route, which relies on cues such as emotions, visuals, and source attractiveness. Emotional appeals in sustainability campaigns function as peripheral cues that capture attention and evoke empathy, concern, or urgency regarding sustainability issues.

3.5: Exposure to Sustainability Communication Positively Influences Participation in Sustainability Activities

Exposure significantly influenced participation in sustainability-related activities ($\beta = 0.634$, $p < 0.001$), accounting for 22.9% of the variance in participation ($R^2 = 0.229$). students with higher exposure to sustainability communication were more likely to engage in activities such as awareness campaigns, educational initiatives, and environmental programs. The finding supports the proposition that media communication can stimulate civic engagement and participation. However, the comparatively lower mean score for participation suggests the existence of a knowledge action gap. Although students demonstrate awareness and positive attitudes towards sustainability, translating these attitudes into actual participation remains challenging due to practical constraints, social norms, or limited opportunities for engagement. The fact that greater internet knowledge does not always translate into real sustainable conduct (Soni et al., 2021).

Predictor	**Beta**	**t-value**	**p-value**	**Significance**
Constant	—	—	—	—
Exposure	0.155	2.22	0.028	Significant
Storytelling	0.770	7.35	<0.001	Highly Significant
Visual Appeal	-0.031	-0.39	0.695	Not Significant

Table 1. Multiple Regression Results- Dependent Variable: SDG Recall

- $R^2 = 0.460$
- Adjusted $R^2 = 0.452$
- F-statistic significant at $p < 0.001$

4. Conclusion:

The significant relationship between exposure and SDG recall (H1) supports Bandura's proposition that repeated exposure to media models enhances learning and retention. Similarly, the positive influence of exposure on participation in sustainability-related activities (H5) suggests that media content can motivate behavioural responses through observational learning.

The strong influence of storytelling on SDG recall (H2) further reinforces Bandura's notion that learning becomes more effective when information is embedded within relatable social situations. Narrative-based communication allows students to identify with characters, observe problem-solving processes, and internalize sustainability values. This finding resonates with educational media research demonstrating that narrative role models facilitate cognitive and behavioural learning.

Jenkins' Participatory Culture Theory (2006) provides an additional explanation for these findings within contemporary digital environments. Jenkins argues that audiences are no longer passive consumers of media but active participants who engage with, interpret, and circulate content. The effectiveness of storytelling can therefore be attributed not only to message exposure but also to the deeper engagement it fosters. Sustainability narratives encourage students to connect media messages with their own experiences, thereby strengthening recall and understanding. The significant effects of visual appeal and emotional appeal (H3 and H4) can also be understood through participatory engagement, as emotionally resonant and visually compelling content captures attention and promotes cognitive involvement.

Most importantly, the analysis identified storytelling as the strongest predictor of SDG recall, while visual appeal has limited significance when storytelling was included. This suggests that meaningful narratives, rather than visuals alone, drive learning outcomes. Together, Bandura's Social Learning Theory and Jenkins' Participatory Culture Theory explain how students learn sustainability concepts through observation, engagement, and active interpretation of digital media content such as Meena.

Students exposed to Meena's narratives may internalize these messages through observational learning, leading to improved understanding and recall of sustainability concepts. A move towards sustainable consumerism is frequently the result of social media platforms' increased environmental knowledge and sense of responsibility (Horrich et al., 2025). When it comes to healthy habits, children learn fundamental hygienic practices during their early years. A lifetime of healthy living is built on good habits such as washing your hands, staying hydrated, and eating a balanced diet (Mitchell, et al., 2021). The evaluations also reported positive effects on behavioural intentions, with participants expressing greater willingness to postpone early marriage and support the education of their female siblings (UNICEF, 2005). Children listening to Meena Radio, 100% of them recalled at least one message instantly (Meena ki Duniya, UNICEF, 2013).

However, lack of access to electricity, internet connectivity, computers, smart phones and data amongst some families inhibited many students from accessing remote learning (Manyengo, 2021) and access to digital tools and technologies. Considering accessibility gaps and digital divide in the country, schools and educational institutes might include Meena Communication Initiative and entertainment education in community set ups.

5. Limitations of the study:

The study has several limitations that should be considered while interpreting the findings. The research adopted a cross-sectional survey design, which captures respondents' perceptions at a single point in time and therefore limits the ability to establish causal relationships between sustainability communication and behavioural outcomes. Furthermore, the sample was restricted to a specific group of students, which may affect the generalizability of the findings to other age and peer groups, cultural settings, or geographical contexts.

6. References:

- Bandura, A., & McDonald, F. J. (1963). Influence of social reinforcement and the behavior of models in shaping children's moral judgment. *Journal of Abnormal and Social Psychology, 67*(3), 274–281.

- Bouman, M. (1999). *The turtle and the peacock: Collaboration for prosocial change. The entertainment-education strategy on television* (Doctoral dissertation, Wageningen University). https://library.wur.nl/WebQuery/wurpubs/fulltext/164907

- Bouman, M. (2002). Turtles and peacocks: Collaboration in entertainment-education television. *Communication Theory, 12*(2), 225–244. https://doi.org/10.1111/j.1468-2885.2002.tb00268.x

- Bouman, M. (2015). *Entertainment media for behaviour change training program*. http://www.media-gezondheid.nl/beheer/data/cmg.desh26.nl/uploads/Bhutan_Nuffic/Entertainment_Media_for_Behaviour_Change_Nuffic_Bhutan_reportAug2015_CMH_fin.pdf

- Bouman, M. (2016). *Amusing ourselves to health and happiness* (pp. 1–18). Erasmus Research Centre for Media, Communication and Culture, Center for Media & Health, & Netherlands Entertainment-Education Foundation.

- Castells, M. (2008). The new public sphere: Global civil society, communication networks, and global governance. *The Annals of the American Academy of Political and Social Science, 616*(1), 78–93. https://doi.org/10.1177/0002716207311877

- Chatterjee, J. S., Sangalang, A., & Cody, M. J. (2017). Entertainment-education. In P. Rössler, C. A. Hoffner, & L. van Zoonen (Eds.), *The international encyclopedia of media effects* (pp. 1–12). John Wiley & Sons. https://doi.org/10.1002/9781118783764.wbieme0067

- Chatterjee, N., et al. (2018). Meena and the changing face of girls' empowerment in South Asia. *Journal of Development Communication, 29*(2), 45–60.

- Chesterton, P. (2004). *Evaluation of the Meena Communication Initiative*. UNICEF Regional Office for South Asia. https://www.unicef.org/evaldatabase/files/ROSA_2004_800_Meena_Comm_Initiative.pdf

- Green, M. C., & Brock, T. C. (2005). Persuasiveness of narratives. In T. C. Brock & M. C. Green (Eds.), *Persuasion: Psychological insights and perspectives* (pp. 117–142). Sage Publications.

- Hoffner, C., & Buchanan, M. (2005). Young adults' wishful identification with television characters. *Media Psychology, 7*(4), 325–351.

- Horrich, A., Ertz, M., & Bekir, I. (2025). Exploring the role of social media in shaping sustainable consumer behavior: A qualitative study. *Cogent Business & Management, 12*(1), Article 2560648. https://doi.org/10.1080/23311975.2025.2560648

- Ihsaniyati, H., Sarwoprasodjo, S., Muljono, P., & Gandasari, D. (2023). The use of social media for development communication and social change: A review. *Sustainability, 15*(3), Article 2283. https://doi.org/10.3390/su15032283

- Jenkins, H. (2006). *Convergence culture: Where old and new media collide*. New York University Press.
- Kauffman, L. E., Dura, E. A., & Borzekowski, D. L. G. (2022). Emotions, strategies, and health: Examining the impact of an educational program on Tanzanian preschool children. *International Journal of Environmental Research and Public Health, 19*(10), Article 5884. https://doi.org/10.3390/ijerph19105884
- Lutkenhaus, R. (2020). *Entertainment education in the new media landscape* (ERMeCC Doctoral Dissertations, Vol. 21). Erasmus Research Centre for Media, Communication and Culture.
- Manyengo, P. R. (2021). *Digitalization in teaching and education in the United Republic of Tanzania: Digitalization, the future of work and the teaching profession project*. International Labour Organization.
- McCorry, K., Maniatopoulos, G., et al. (2026). Recognizing the importance of design, content, and delivery features of health animations for preventive health behaviors: Realist review. *Journal of Medical Internet Research, 28*, e79769. https://doi.org/10.2196/79769
- Mitchell, A. E., Kulasinghe, K., & Morawska, A. (2021). Establishing healthy personal hygiene habits with young children in Australia: A cross-sectional mixed methods study. *Behaviour Change*.

- Nabavi, R. T., & Bijandi, M. S. (2012). *Bandura's social learning theory & social cognitive learning theory* [Literature review]. ResearchGate. https://www.researchgate.net/publication/267750204_Bandura's_Social_Learning_Theory_Social_Cognitive_Learning_Theory

- Petty, R. E., & Cacioppo, J. T. (1986). The elaboration likelihood model of persuasion. In R. E. Petty & J. T. Cacioppo (Eds.), *Communication and persuasion: Central and peripheral routes to attitude change* (pp. 1–24). Springer. https://doi.org/10.1007/978-1-4612-4964-1_1

- Scolari, C. A. (2009). Transmedia storytelling: Implicit consumers, narrative worlds, and branding in contemporary media production. *International Journal of Communication, 3*, 586–606.

- Servaes, J. (Ed.). (2020). *Handbook of communication for development and social change*. Springer.

- Singhal, A., & Rogers, E. M. (2002). A theoretical agenda for entertainment-education. *Communication Theory, 12*(2), 117–135. https://doi.org/10.1111/j.1468-2885.2002.tb00262.x

- Singhal, A., & Rogers, E. M. (2004). The status of entertainment-education worldwide. In A. Singhal, M. J. Cody, E. M. Rogers, & M. Sabido (Eds.), *Entertainment-education and social change* (pp. 3–18). Lawrence Erlbaum Associates.

- Soni, M., Dawar, S., & Soni, A. (2021). Probing consumer awareness and barriers towards consumer social responsibility: A novel sustainable development approach. *International Journal of Sustainable Development and Planning,* *16*(1), 89–96. https://doi.org/10.18280/ijsdp.160109

- UNICEF Regional Office for South Asia. (2001). *Meeting Meena: Documentation study on utilisation of Meena Communication Initiative*. United Nations Children's Fund.

- Van Evra, J. (2004). *Television and child development* (3rd ed.). Routledge.

- Vandormael, A., Adam, M., Greuel, M., Gates, J., Favaretti, C., Hachaturyan, V., & Bärnighausen, T. (2021). The effect of a wordless, animated, social media video intervention on COVID-19 prevention: Online randomized controlled trial. *JMIR Public Health and Surveillance,* *7*(7), e29060. https://doi.org/10.2196/29060

- Wang, L. (2018). Book review: Henry Jenkins, Mimi Ito and danah boyd, *Participatory culture in a networked era*. *Global Media and China,* *3*(1), 1–4. https://doi.org/10.1177/2059436418771394

- UNICEF. (2013). *Meena Ki Duniya: An entertainment-education radio initiative—The production process*. https://global.comminit.com/files/meenabookfinal.pdf

CHAPTER 6

Bridging Trust Gaps and Reputation Management: Health Communication Across Public and Private Sectors

Dr. Ananya Mehta

Abstract: In today's highly mediated healthcare landscape, trust and reputation are vital assets shaped by strategic communication efforts. This chapter explores how both the public and private healthcare sectors use communication strategies to manage risk, establish credibility, and maintain their reputations amid complex regulatory and informational environments. Going beyond simple information-sharing models, it emphasises health communication as a key aspect of public relations that manages relationships between organisations, stakeholders, and the public.

Using secondary data and international case studies, the analysis aims to show that public healthcare institutions tend to depend on uniform, policy-focused messaging to gain legitimacy and ensure compliance. In contrast, private players employ more active reputation management tactics, such as branding, personalised interactions, and digital storytelling. These distinct strategies affect how risk is portrayed, transparency is understood, and ultimately, how trust is built or damaged among different audiences.

The chapter seeks to further explore the role of social media platforms, where visibility, stakeholder feedback, and real-time engagement can make or break an institution's reputation. In such environments, ineffective or inconsistent communication can deepen trust deficits, particularly in high-risk health contexts. Conversely, strategic, audience-centred communication can enhance credibility, mitigate misinformation, and strengthen long-term relationships.

This chapter advocates for a more integrated approach to health and risk communication from a public relations standpoint, emphasising ethical responsibility, message consistency, and stakeholder engagement. Closing trust gaps involves not just providing accurate information but also ongoing reputation management that is responsive, transparent, and culturally sensitive throughout healthcare sectors.

Keywords: *Public Relations, Reputation & Trust, Health Communication, Private & Public Healthcare*

1. Conceptual Framework

Health communication has evolved from merely providing information to a strategic public relations (PR) practice that influences trust, credibility, and institutional reputation. In modern healthcare systems, communication plays a key role in shaping how patients perceive risks, evaluate service quality, and interact with providers. Trust remains a vital element in this relationship, influencing patients' adherence to medical advice and their willingness to engage with healthcare organisations. (Cantarutti & Pothos, 2021).

From a PR perspective, health communication extends beyond message delivery; it serves as a system for managing relationships between healthcare organisations and their stakeholders. While traditional behaviour-change models such as the Health Belief Model and the Theory of Planned Behaviour continue to influence message design, recent research highlights socio-ecological approaches that emphasise community involvement and cultural context. (Aghazadeh & Aldoory, 2023).

Within this framework, risk communication becomes a key PR activity. Communicating uncertainty, managing perceptions of safety, and maintaining credibility require coordinated strategies across multiple platforms. As healthcare systems become increasingly digital and market-driven, the management of trust and reputation has become inseparable from communication practice.

2. Trust, Risk, and the Role of Communication

Trust in healthcare is established through perceptions of competence, reliability, transparency, and empathy. Inconsistent or delayed communication can quickly erode trust, harming both the institution's reputation and patient results. Studies indicate that communication quality strongly predicts public satisfaction, and communication failures are a major source of complaints (Rayner et al., 2025).

Risk communication further complicates this relationship. Healthcare organizations must convey uncertainty carefully, avoiding the amplification of fear through thoughtful message framing, clarity, and responsiveness. Effective risk communication often determines whether an institution appears trustworthy or unreliable. Meanwhile, digital platforms have heightened communication challenges, as many people now access health information online, encountering both credible data and misinformation (Fridman et al., 2023). The World Health Organization highlights misinformation and disinformation as major public health threats because they can undermine trust in institutions and lead to harmful decisions (World Health Organization, 2024).

From a PR standpoint, this reinforces the need for proactive communication strategies focused on transparency, responsiveness, and continuous engagement.

3. Communication Strategies in Public and Private Healthcare

A key difference in healthcare communication exists between the public and private sectors. Although both sectors seek to inform and involve stakeholders, they vary notably in their motivations, limitations, and communication approaches.

Public healthcare institutions usually function within regulatory frameworks that emphasize standardization and accountability to the public. Their communication methods tend to be formal, policy-oriented, and aimed at maintaining consistency. However, this approach can create one-way communication, limiting engagement and responsiveness. Researchers suggest that these' command-and-control' strategies may undermine public trust if they do not include community viewpoints. (Steiner & Yasmin, 2025).

In contrast, private healthcare organisations operate in competitive environments, which lead to significant investments in branding, stakeholder engagement, and reputation management. Their communication strategies act as key differentiators, showcasing service quality, patient experience, and innovation. Branding is especially vital in forming perceptions, building emotional bonds, and cultivating patient loyalty (Faster Capital, 2024).

The following table summarizes key differences:

Table 1. Commonly Used Communication Characteristics Across Healthcare Sectors

Dimension	Public Healthcare	Private Healthcare
Communication orientation	Policy and compliance	Market and relationship oriented
Message style	Standardised, formal	Personalised, persuasive
Engagement model	Top-down dissemination	Interactive engagement
Reputation logic	Legitimacy and trust	Brand-driven trust
Channel use	Institutional platforms	Digital and social media

These differences influence how risk is communicated, how transparency is perceived, and how trust is constructed among stakeholders.

4. Digital Media, Reputation, and Communication Risk

Digital platforms have reshaped healthcare communication into a constant, "always-on" PR setting. Although these platforms expand reach and boost engagement, they also create potential reputation risks.

Healthcare communication now takes place through various channels such as websites, mobile apps, and social media. For instance, National Health Service (NHS) England launched a unified messaging system that handled over 257 million interactions with patients, enhancing access while also underscoring the need for consistency and coordination in communication platforms.

Despite these developments, the digital landscape heightens certain risks. Social media enables patients to openly share their experiences, critique healthcare services, and shape public opinion instantly. Studies on healthcare communication emphasise the importance of the CARE model—Control, Access, Responsiveness, and Engagement—for safeguarding online reputation (Chaudhri et al., 2021).

Misinformation poses an additional challenge. Incorrect or misleading health information spreads rapidly online and can erode institutional credibility. This creates a paradox in which greater access to information does not necessarily lead to better-informed audiences. Instead, organisations must actively engage in digital spaces to maintain authority and trust.

5. Reputation Management and Strategic Communication

Reputation in healthcare develops over time through ongoing communication efforts rather than single campaigns. It indicates how reliably organisations share their values, address stakeholder concerns, and handle crises.

A prime example of strategic reputation management is the Cleveland Clinic, which shifted its communication focus to a "Patients First" philosophy. By emphasising patient experience and empathy in its messaging, the organisation enhanced its international reputation and boosted patient satisfaction results.

Cleveland Clinic faced challenges making a favourable impression in a competitive healthcare market with many options. Even with its outstanding clinical care, it struggled to clearly convey its unique value to patients, who often viewed healthcare as just a simple transaction rather than a meaningful, transformative journey.

A strategic rebranding exercise was undertaken to improve the patient experience and manage the clinic's reputation. The Cleveland Clinic's extensive rebranding effort aimed to enhance the patient experience by going beyond clinical services to build emotional bonds. The organisation invested in empathy training, revamped patient interactions, and reoriented its brand messaging around the principle of "Patients First. "

The positive patient experience initiative began with an emphasis on empathy, fundamentally changing Cleveland Clinic's approach to patient interactions. This was more than just a visual identity update; it signified a comprehensive shift in organisational culture.

Likewise, studies on hospital branding show that clear communication strategies can build trust, set services apart, and foster lasting stakeholder relationships. (Medina Aguerrebere et al., 2021).

From a PR perspective, reputation management in healthcare involves:

- Consistent messaging across platforms
- Transparent communication of risks and uncertainties
- Active stakeholder engagement
- Monitoring and responding to public feedback

Reputation is influenced not just by what organisations communicate, but also by their responses to challenges and criticism.

6. Bridging Trust Gaps: Toward Integrated PR Approaches

Bridging trust gaps between healthcare institutions and stakeholders involves implementing integrated communication strategies that merge public relations principles with health communication theories.

Initially, transparency should be emphasised. Clear communication about uncertainties and limitations builds trust and helps prevent misinformation. Next, maintaining consistency across all channels guarantees that stakeholders get uniform messages, which minimises confusion and doubt. Lastly, adopting engagement-oriented communication rather than one-way messaging allows organizations to better address community needs and expectations.

Cultural sensitivity remains crucial in global healthcare. Effective communication requires tailoring strategies to various populations by considering language, cultural values, and access to media. Additionally, enhancing digital health literacy is vital for helping audiences interpret complex information.

These approaches align with modern PR principles, which prioritise relationship-building, co-creating meaning, and sustained engagement over quick persuasion.

7. Conclusion

Health communication plays a vital role in building trust, managing risks, and maintaining reputation within modern healthcare systems. Although the public and private sectors employ different communication strategies, they both encounter challenges such as digital transformation, misinformation, and changing stakeholder expectations. This study focuses that communication is more than just a support function; it is a strategic tool that influences institutional legitimacy and public involvement. Closing trust gaps requires moving from simple informational models to integrated, audience-focused communication approaches grounded in public relations principles. Ultimately, healthcare organizations that focus on transparency, responsiveness, and engagement will be in a stronger position to maintain trust and build their reputations, especially as communication environments become more complex. By embracing these values, they can foster stronger connections with those they serve and navigate challenges more effectively.

References

- Aghazadeh, S. A., & Aldoory, L. (2023). Health communication theory in public relations. In E. L. Toth & C. H. Botan (Eds.), *Public relations theory III: In the age of publics* (pp. 395–411). Routledge. https://doi.org/10.4324/9781003141396-27
- Accelabrand. (2025, September 3). *5 healthcare rebranding case studies that drove measurable ROI in 2025*. https://accelabrand.com/5-healthcare-rebranding-case-studies/
- Cantarutti, S., & Pothos, E. M. (2023). How healthcare structures and communication delivery influence trust: A parallel-group randomized controlled trial. *Journal of Public*

Health, 31(6), 831–836. https://doi.org/10.1007/s10389-021-01620-z

- Chaudhri, V., de Bruijne, M., Pridmore, J., & Joon, A. (2021). CARE in social media: Perceptions of reputation in the healthcare sector. *Journal of Communication Management, 25*(2), 125–141. https://doi.org/10.1108/JCOM-06-2020-0059
- FasterCapital. (2024). *Private hospital branding strategies*. FasterCapital. https://fastercapital.com
- Fridman, I., Johnson, S., & Lafata, J. E. (2023). Health information and misinformation: A framework to guide research and practice. *JMIR Medical Education, 9*, e38687. https://doi.org/10.2196/38687
- Medina Aguerrebere, P., González Pacanowski, T., & Medina, E. (2021). Building meaningful brands through social media: A case study about hospitals. *Harvard Deusto Business Research, 10*(1), 176–189. https://doi.org/10.48132/hdbr.342
- Rayner, H., Collins, A., Hewitt, P., & McDonald, A. (2025). Poor communication with patients erodes trust in the NHS. *BMJ, 389*, r947. https://doi.org/10.1136/bmj.r947
- Steiner, R., & Yasmin, S. (2025). Restoring trust in public health: Communications lessons from person-centered health care. *European Journal*

of Public Health, 35(Supplement_2), ii9–ii10. https://doi.org/10.1093/eurpub/ckae151

- Vlasiadis, K., Vlasiadis, Z., & Kliagkona, K. (2025). Public relations and communication in healthcare facilities. [Unable to verify publication details in Crossref, Scopus, Web of Science, PubMed, or Google Scholar. Please provide the DOI, URL, publisher, or journal title.]

- World Health Organization. (2024, February 6). *Disinformation and public health*. World Health Organization.

https://www.who.int/news-room/questions-and-answers/item/disinformation-and-public-health

CHAPTER 7

Borrowing Humanity: Human Libraries as Strategic Communication Ecosystems for Empathy, Trust, and Social Transformation

Mehakdeep Kaur

Abstract: In an algorithmically dominated communication ecosystem where speed and visibility are often prioritized over depth and dialogue, the question of how meaningful human communication can survive, let alone thrive, becomes increasingly pressing. The Human Library, first developed in Copenhagen in 2000, offers a compelling example of a communicative practice built around direct encounter, structured storytelling, and the challenge of prejudice. This chapter examines the Human Library as a strategic communication phenomenon with implications for social transformation and communication for social change. Drawing on dialogic communication theory, the narrative paradigm, and participatory approaches to communication, it argues that the Human Library works not by maximizing reach, but by creating conditions for empathy, trust, and reflective listening. The chapter situates the Human Library within broader debates on platform culture and the commodification of attention, showing how face-to-face dialogue can expose the limitations of data-driven visibility and re-center authentic communication. It concludes that strategic communication research should engage more seriously with models of direct engagement such as the Human Library, where sustainable social change depends not only on persuasive messages but also on good listening.

Keywords: *Human Library; strategic communication; dialogic communication; communication for social change; empathy; platform culture*

1. Introduction

The definition of public interaction has shifted with digital communication. Now, messages pass through platforms that are designed to gauge, rank, and pay for attention, and in which values of speed, sentiment and perpetual presence outweigh values of reflection and mutual understanding. Within this context, success of communication is often measured by the extent of reach, engagement, and circulation. However, these indicators do not necessarily reflect whether communication has helped to enhance understanding, diminish prejudice or improve social trust. That is why the field of strategic communication needs to pose a harder question, though: What kinds of communication still make for meaningful human connection in a platform-dominated world?

The Human Library is one solution. The Human Library was conceived in Copenhagen in 2000, as a social innovation that allows people to "borrow" another human being for a conversation, akin to the way that a reader borrows a book from a traditional library. The purpose of the initiative is to tackle prejudice and promote conversation around difference, by providing an opportunity to engage with people whose identity or experiences are mistaken, stigmatised or stereotyped. As described by the Human Library Organization, the project is a library of people in which one can engage in conversations with books in a respectful, organized space.

The Human Library should be considered a strategic communication ecosystem, this chapter contends. It's not just an event format or novelty, it's a structured model of communication that structures relationships, narratives and social learning around direct engagement. The Human Library values understanding rather than campaign models that focus on the delivery of messages and digital models that focus on engagement figures. It provides a place for stories, questions, listening and curiosity to be able to interrupt prejudice and elicit empathy.

It is based on the Dialogic Communication Theory and the theory of the Human Library, which is based on Fisher's narrative paradigm and participatory communication for social change, to explain the concept and the social significance of the Human Library. Kent and Taylor's dialogue in public relations focus on the values of dialogue, namely mutuality, empathy, and relational engagement. Fisher's concept of the narrative paradigm reveals human perception of the world in terms of stories and the assessment of messages based on their narrative coherence and fidelity. The participatory communication scholarship also holds that communication processes which involve dialogue, local meaning-making and participation are needed to create social change, rather than one-way transmissions. These frameworks can help to shed light on the potential for the Human Library as a strategic and humane communication practice.

2. The Human Library as a Communication Form

The Human Library is at first very simple. It's like a traditional library, except that the participants borrow lived experience speakers rather than printed books. The "books" may be people who have been labeled as having a stigma, prejudice, or misunderstanding based on their identity, occupation, history, or circumstances. The "readers" choose a book from a catalogue and engage in an interaction with the book's author for a fixed period of time. Rules are in place to foster respect, openness and curiosity in the interaction.

This format is important because it shifts the way students think about reading as a relational process. The reader meets up with a text in a traditional library. The Human Library is a book in which the reader meets a person. This change alters the definition of knowledge. It's not just a fact sheet on a social group; it's a person who can set the record straight and give an inside view on a lived experience. The Human Library is pedagogical and ethical in this regard. It teaches by making the human.It teaches by humanising.

The Human Library is also based on curation. Book presentation, conversational parameters, and conditions for safe exchange are determined by organizers. This is significant since dialogue does not just naturally follow contact. Contact can result in misunderstandings when it is unstructured or can be hostile. The Human Library, therefore, employs design as a means of communication. It creates a context in which "difference" can be examined without making the "book" into a "symbol" or the "reader" into an "object.

Human Libraries have been used in schools, universities, festivals, public libraries and community spaces over the years. The way they are spreading shows they are satisfying a need that is widely felt: for places that allow people to pose sincere questions about difference without fear of ridicule; for opportunities and places that allow for the structures that enable marginalized people to speak for themselves instead of being spoken about. The Human Library is so compelling because it is an idea that helps bridge the gap between these needs.

3. Theoretical Grounding

3.1.Dialogic communication

One of the most useful theories of dialogue is the theory of dialogic communication which is developed by the Human Library. The concepts of dialogue as developed by Kent and Taylor in the field of public relations do not simply refer to a passing of messages, but to a relational approach characterized by the concepts of mutuality, propinquity, empathy, risk, and commitment. Mutuality is acknowledging the other person as a legitimate communicator. Propinquity is the ability to communicate in a timely, immediate and accessible manner. Empathy is having a glimpse of another person's point of view. Risk admits that true conversation involves being vulnerable. Commitment implies staying in the relationship for the long haul, not just for the short term or to benefit one partner.

These values are put into action in The Human Library. Readers and books meet as individuals rather than types. It's a person-to-person interaction, no delays. Often personal experiences are revealed in books to be vulnerable, and reader's may be at risk of encountering assumptions they may wish to hold. The event is also designed to help move beyond the saccharine politeness. Dialogic is not about dialogue, but about providing conditions which allow dialogue to happen; in this sense, the Human Library is dialogic.

The dialogic perspective is particularly valuable because it helps to focus the attention from persuasion as a one-way process. In many strategic communications situations, the intent is to create meaningful messages that impact behaviors or attitudes. The Human Library proposes a different way of communicating that is strategic: reciprocal understanding. It is not about giving up influence, but instead about changing what influence is from message control to relational transformation.

3.2.Narrative paradigm

A second paradigm is provided by Fisher's narrative paradigm. Fisher contended that people are basically storytellers and that stories form the main way of understanding reality. From this perspective, audiences rate stories on their coherence and fidelity - a story should be internally coherent, and it should ring true to the listener's lived experience or sense of truth. Stories are convincing not only because they are logically presented, but because they seem to be a part of something, something that is morally defensible.

The Human Library will rely on storytelling. Every human book is a book of difference, struggle, resilience and identity. These stories are not merely arguments about social categories: they are lived stories, places for readers to experience the complexities of human life. Replacing generalization with specificity is one of the ways that a single conversation can challenge a stereotype. When a reader hears a lived story, the category doesn't seem so closed or simple.

The Human Library can also be effective without having reached a large audience through the media, something that can be understood by the narrative paradigm. The strength of the model is not the number of samples, but the depth of the model. Repeated exposure to mediated messaging may be less effective than a story told in person in an environment that allows the listener to give attention and respect to the story. There is a strong tendency to assume that strategic communication needs to be scaled up in order to have an impact. Intimacy can be transformative too as demonstrated by The Human Library.

3.3. Participatory communication for social change

A third framework is participatory communication. Communication for social change approaches negate the notion of development or change being delivered as a message from above to passive audiences. On the contrary, they emphasize local participation, horizontal exchange and collective meaning making. Communication becomes a place of speaking, listening, co-creating understanding.

The Human Library is very much in tune with this tradition. Human books are not just information sources, they are contributors to the conversation. Readers are not passive but ask questions and manipulate the exchange. The organizers create conditions, do not determine meaning. Because it generates a participatory model where social changes are the result of social interaction.

This is so because information is not usually enough to alter prejudice. Social change tends to necessitate encounter, reflexivity and the opportunity to hear difference in a human voice. The Human Library puts participation at the heart of the action, by connecting individuals who may be divided by social barriers. Does not imply that every disagreement can be resolved by consensus. Rather, it adopts communication as a means to render the social world 'listenable'.

4. Platform Culture and Attention

The Human Library can have greater meaning when considered in a platform culture context. In digital platforms, attention economies are enacted wherein the ability to measure and monetise the significance of visibility is valued. Quickly accessible, emotionally evocative, or highly shareable material is preferred by these systems. Therefore, the idea of communication is more and more occurring in a context in which attention is split and understanding is secondary.

This is relevant to strategic communication. Organizations are sometimes driven to pursue an engagement metric as an indicator of social impact. However, there is a difference between engagement and understanding. A post can be viewed by a lot of people and not change the prejudice. For a campaign to build awareness, it must also establish trust. The Human Library reveals this disparity by demonstrating that development of meaningful communication may occur in an intangible place.

The model thus provides a critique on the logic of platforms while not necessarily opposing digital communication. It's not saying technology is evil, or that online is not working. Instead, it uncovers what digital systems haven't got the capacity for: silent listening, waiting patiently to ask questions, and personal accountability. One of the most vital forms of social communication are not the most obvious ones, as the Human Library shows.

It also implies that attention should be comprehended in an ethical way, and not merely an economic way. In a Human Library, the attention isn't taken away by an algorithm but given freely and freely given back. The difference is important because when ethical attention is present, so is the possibility for trust. In this way, when people don't feel harvested, they aren't harvested, and communication is more human and less instrumental.

5. Empathy, Trust, and Social Transformation

Empathy is part of the core of the Human Library's social value. The format is an invitation to go beyond labels and understand. But here, empathy is not a sentimental identification, which is important. It's a disciplined willingness to hear and leave behind one's assumptions. In this respect, empathy is emotional and cognitive: it is the ability to feel what others feel and at the same time, to understand one's own perspective is not all-encompassing.

Trust is born of the same process. Books are believed by readers, readers are believed by books. The transformative potential of the encounter is due to these two vulnerabilities. People may have prejudices and they may avoid contact with those they stereotype. The Human Library steps in and provides a safe space for the exchange itself.

A transition from abstraction to specificity is a common communicative effect. A reader might have a general conception of a group prior to the encounter. Once the encounter has taken place, the group is no longer a category, it is linked to a specific human being, with a voice, a history and a point of view. It can make it more difficult to maintain prejudice as some anonymity of stereotypes is lost. The reader is now acquainted with a character who challenges a false image.

The Human Library, on the other hand, is not to be romanticized. Re-telling a painful story may be difficult for marginalized people. There is also a danger that readers would be reading books to find out something new, instead of reading them like an equal. So, ethical facilitation is important. A Human Library is not just a story-sharing, it is also a story sharing that is carefully, bounded, and respectful.

6. Strategic Communication Implications

The Human Library offers a number of implications for strategic communication theory and practice. Firstly, it broadens the field's concept of strategy. The word strategy is usually linked to planning, persuading, targeting and optimizing messages. Beyond having a specific strategy, strategy is also the design of relational conditions, according to the Human Library, for an understanding to become possible. Communication strategy is not limited to what is said but also how people are brought together in this sense.

Second, it emphasises the need for listening. Strategic communication tends to favour speaking, broadcasting and message control. But for the social transformation to be sustainable, one must be receptive. Listening is a communicative act, so it is not just a passive act, it is an active act, it demands attention, humility, responsiveness. The Human Library demonstrates that listening can be a type of intervention.

Thirdly, it puts the researcher to a challenge to think about alternative criteria for evaluation. A successful Human Library may not have measurable impacts, but it can make a big difference when it impacts an attitude, feeling or behavior towards difference. It might be better to assess such impact using qualitative measures, reflective statements and narrative feedback than just metrics.

Third, the Human Library serves as a model for the hybrid communication design. Digital tools can support the organization, promotion and scale of such experiences, but the communicative experience must still be a human one. The point of the lesson is not to give up on digital platforms, but to not give them their whole meaning.

7. Conclusion

The Human Library is a powerful example of communication designed for empathy, trust, and social transformation. What makes it significant is not only its creativity, but its refusal to reduce communication to visibility metrics. By enabling structured conversation between people who might otherwise remain separated by prejudice, the Human Library creates a space where stories can humanize and dialogue can unsettle stereotypes.

Seen through dialogic communication theory, the narrative paradigm, and participatory communication for social change, the Human

Library becomes more than an event. It becomes a communication ecosystem that values mutuality, narrative meaning, and participatory exchange. In a platform culture that often commodifies attention, this model reminds us that social transformation depends on more than persuasive messages. It depends on the human capacity to listen, encounter, and revise what we think we know.

For strategic communication scholarship, the Human Library offers a timely lesson: the future of meaningful communication may lie not in speaking louder, but in creating better spaces for people to hear one another.

References:

- Bagci, S. C., & Blazhenkova, O. (2020). Unjudge someone: Human Library as a tool to reduce prejudice toward stigmatized group members. *Basic and Applied Social Psychology, 42*(6), 413–431. https://doi.org/10.1080/01973533.2020.1792298
- Bolton-Fasman, J. (2026, April 28). *In the Human Library Organization, people are books to be read.* WBUR Cognoscenti. https://www.wbur.org/cognoscenti
- Couldry, N., & Mejias, U. A. (2019). *The costs of connection: How data is colonizing human life and appropriating it for capitalism.* Stanford University Press.
- Fisher, W. R. (1984). Narration as a human communication paradigm: The case of public

moral argument. *Communication Monographs, 51*(1), 1–22. https://doi.org/10.1080/03637758409390180

- Freire, P. (1983). *Pedagogy of the oppressed* (M. B. Ramos, Trans.). Continuum. (Original work published 1970)
- Gerbaudo, P. (2012). *Tweets and the streets: Social media and contemporary activism*. Pluto Press.
- Groyecka, A., Ledzińska, M., Żółtak, T., & Żadkowska, M. (2019). Human Library as a method of reducing prejudice and social distance. *Current Issues in Personality Psychology, 7*(4), 287–297. https://doi.org/10.5114/cipp.2019.89180
- Hjarvard, S. (2008). The mediatization of society: A theory of the media as agents of social and cultural change. *Nordicom Review, 29*(2), 105–134. https://doi.org/10.1515/nor-2017-0181
- Human Library Organization. (2020, August 7). *Unjudge someone at the Human Library*. https://humanlibrary.org/unjudge-someone-at-the-human-library/
- Human Library Organization. (2023). *About the Human Library*. https://humanlibrary.org
- Human Library Organization. (2026). *Unjudge someone*. https://humanlibrary.org
- Kent, M. L., & Taylor, M. (1998). Building dialogic relationships through the World Wide Web. *Public Relations Review, 24*(3), 321–334.

https://doi.org/10.1016/S0363-8111(99)80143-X

- Kent, M. L., & Taylor, M. (2002). Toward a dialogic theory of public relations. *Public Relations Review, 28*(1), 21–37. https://doi.org/10.1016/S0363-8111(02)00108-X

- Kent, M. L., & Taylor, M. (2020). Moving forward the dialogic theory of public relations: Concepts, methods, and applications of organization–public dialogue. *Public Relations Review, 46*(1), 101878. https://doi.org/10.1016/j.pubrev.2019.101878

- Kent, M. L., & Theunissen, P. (2016). Between dialogue and dissemination: A model for strategic public relations in the public sphere. *Public Relations Review, 42*(4), 628–635. https://doi.org/10.1016/j.pubrev.2015.07.005

- Kudo, K., Motohashi, Y., & Enomoto, Y. (2011). Effectiveness of a Human Library intervention in changing attitudes toward people with mental illness among university students. *Psychiatry and Clinical Neurosciences, 65*(Suppl. 1), S84–S85.

- Orosz, G., Brunyánszki, A., & Bőthe, B. (2016). The Human Library method as an educational tool to reduce prejudice. *Journal of Applied Social Psychology, 46*(10), 577–587. https://doi.org/10.1111/jasp.12392

- Rahman, A. (1993). *People's self-development: Perspectives on participatory action research*. Zed Books.
- Servaes, J. (1999). *Communication for development: One world, multiple cultures*. Hampton Press.
- Servaes, J. (2008). Communication for development and social change. *Journal of Development Communication, 19*(2), 1–13.
- Servaes, J., & Arnst, R. (1999). Principles of participatory communication research: Its strengths and weaknesses. In J. Servaes (Ed.), *Walking on the other side of the information highway* (pp. 197–217). Southbound.
- Servaes, J., Jacobson, T. L., & White, S. A. (Eds.). (1996). *Participatory communication for social change*. Sage.
- Taylor, M., & Kent, M. L. (2014). Dialogic engagement: Clarifying foundational concepts. *Journal of Public Relations Research, 26*(5), 384–398. https://doi.org/10.1080/1062726X.2014.956106
- Van Dijck, J., Poell, T., & De Waal, M. (2018). *The platform society: Public values in a connective world*. Oxford University Press.
- Walker, L., & Read, S. (2023). Practical tips for using a Human Library approach in medical education to challenge prejudice. *BMC Medical Education, 23*, Article 708. https://doi.org/10.1186/s12909-023-04506-7

CHAPTER 8

The Different Facets of Silence Through Animation Film

Dr. Deepak Sharma, Mr. Indranil Bhattacharya, & Mr. Sujit Kumar Karmakar

Abstract: Silence has emerged as a significant expressive element in cinematic storytelling, particularly within animation films, where every visual and auditory component is intentionally constructed. In animation, silence transcends the simple absence of sound and becomes a sophisticated narrative, psychological, and aesthetic device. This chapter explores how silence functions in animated cinema to communicate emotion, intensify visual storytelling, shape narrative pacing, and enhance audience interpretation. Through theoretical perspectives and detailed analysis of selected animated films such as Wall-E, The Red Turtle, Spirited Away, Grave of the Fireflies, and The Triplets of Belleville, the chapter investigates the emotional, symbolic, and philosophical dimensions of silence in animation. The study also examines cross-cultural approaches to silence, particularly in Japanese, European, and Western animation traditions. Findings suggest that silence enhances emotional immersion, universal accessibility, and contemplative engagement while strengthening the visual power of animated storytelling. The chapter concludes that silence remains an essential cinematic language in contemporary animation and will continue to evolve with emerging technologies such as virtual reality and artificial intelligence-driven storytelling.

Keywords: *Silence, Animation Films, Visual Storytelling, Sound Design, Cinematic Language, Emotional Narrative, Studio Ghibli, Silent Cinema, Psychological Impact, Animation Studies*

1. Introduction

Silence has always occupied a unique and complex position in cinematic language. In film theory, silence is not merely the absence of sound; rather, it is an active aesthetic and narrative strategy capable of shaping emotional responses, constructing meaning, and intensifying visual communication. In animation films, silence becomes even more significant because animation itself is a constructed reality where every gesture, sound, expression, and movement is deliberately designed. Unlike live-action cinema, where silence may emerge naturally from environmental conditions, animated silence is intentional and carefully choreographed. As a result, silence in animation acquires symbolic, psychological, and philosophical dimensions. Bordwell, D., & Thompson, K. (2019)

Animation as a medium is often associated with exaggerated movements, vibrant soundtracks, comic timing, and dynamic dialogue. However, many influential animators and filmmakers have demonstrated that silence can communicate more powerfully than spoken words. Silent moments in animation encourage viewers to observe body language, environmental details, rhythm, pacing, and symbolic imagery. They also create emotional pauses that allow audiences to interpret meanings independently. Through silence, animated films can express loneliness, trauma, love, fear, memory, spirituality, alienation, and contemplation.

According to Michel Chion (1994), silence in film is never entirely silent because audiences continue to perceive emotional tension, environmental presence, and visual rhythm even in the absence of dialogue or music. In animation, silence frequently functions as an expressive contrast to movement and sound, thereby heightening audience engagement and emotional immersion. Chion, M. (1994)

This chapter examines the multiple dimensions of silence in animation films by analyzing its narrative, emotional, psychological, and aesthetic functions. The discussion further explores how filmmakers from different cultural traditions employ silence as a storytelling strategy through selected case studies.

2. Understanding Silence in Animation

2.1 Silence as Cinematic Language

Silence in cinema should not be understood as emptiness. Instead, it acts as a communicative space that allows viewers to experience emotions beyond verbal articulation. In animation, silence often reveals internal conflicts, emotional transitions, or philosophical reflections that dialogue may fail to communicate effectively. Prince, S. (2012).

The language of animation depends heavily upon visual performance. Facial expressions, body movement, framing, colour, lighting, rhythm, and timing become essential tools in silent sequences. Early experiments by Walt Disney demonstrated that audiences could emotionally connect with animated characters even with minimal dialogue. Silent-era animation relied extensively on exaggerated gestures and visual timing, techniques that continue to influence contemporary animated cinema. Wells, P. (1998).

Silence also promotes active audience participation. Rather than receiving direct verbal explanations, viewers are encouraged to interpret the meaning independently through observation and emotional engagement. Consequently, silent animated films often achieve universal accessibility by transcending linguistic barriers. Furniss, M. (2007).

2.2 Psychological Impact of Silence

Psychologically, silence can evoke calmness, fear, anticipation, nostalgia, loneliness, or contemplation. In animation films, silence frequently amplifies emotional sensitivity because audiences become more attentive to visual and symbolic cues.

Research in film psychology suggests that reduced auditory stimulation increases audience concentration on imagery and emotional nuance (Bordwell & Thompson, 2019). Silent sequences create interpretative spaces where viewers project their own emotions onto characters. This phenomenon becomes especially effective in animation because animated figures often function symbolically rather than realistically. Eisenstein, S. (1949).

For example, a silent close-up of a character staring into space may communicate grief more effectively than extensive dialogue. Silence, therefore, acts as an emotional amplifier rather than merely an absence of sound.

3. The Role of Silence In Narrative Construction

3.1 Silence as a Narrative Device

Animation filmmakers frequently use silence to structure narrative progression. Silent moments commonly appear during transitions, emotional turning points, or moments of realization. By interrupting continuous sound or dialogue, silence draws attention to particular scenes and encourages emotional reflection. Miyazaki, H. (Director). (2001).

In Spirited Away, directed by Hayao Miyazaki, silence plays an essential role in depicting Chihiro's psychological transformation. Several scenes contain minimal dialogue, allowing audiences to absorb the mystical atmosphere of the spirit world. The famous train journey sequence creates a meditative emotional state through visual stillness and restrained sound design. Ebert, R. (2008).

Similarly, silence in animated storytelling can communicate alienation and emotional isolation. Characters who cannot express themselves verbally often rely on gestures and actions, creating emotional authenticity through observation rather than explanation.

3.2 Silence and Pacing

Silence significantly influences cinematic pacing. Fast-paced animated films typically rely on continuous sound effects and dialogue to maintain energy, whereas silent sequences slow narrative tempo and create emotional breathing space. Sito, T. (2013).

Films produced by Studio Ghibli frequently utilize the Japanese aesthetic concept of "ma," referring to meaningful emptiness or pauses between actions. These contemplative pauses encourage viewers to emotionally connect with characters and environments.

Scenes depicting wind moving through grass, rainfall, or characters silently observing landscapes contribute to atmospheric depth and emotional realism. Such moments prevent narrative fatigue and intensify emotional resonance. McCloud, S. (1993).

4. Visual Storytelling and Silence

4.1 Expressive Animation without Dialogue

One of animation's greatest strengths lies in visual storytelling. Silent sequences emphasize movement, gesture, composition, and symbolic imagery.

Animators often depend upon exaggerated body language and facial expressions to communicate emotions clearly.

In The Triplets of Belleville, directed by Sylvain Chomet, dialogue is almost entirely minimized. Characters communicate through expressions, visual humour, and rhythmic motion. The absence of verbal communication enhances the film's surreal atmosphere while making it universally accessible. Sito, T. (2013).

Silence directs audience attention toward environmental details, editing rhythms, and visual composition, transforming animation into a highly cinematic visual experience.

4.2 Symbolism and Metaphor

Silence frequently supports symbolic storytelling. Animated films often employ metaphorical imagery to communicate abstract concepts such as memory, death, emotional repression, and spirituality.

Environmental sounds become symbolic extensions of character psychology during silent moments. Wind, rain, footsteps, distant echoes, and waves acquire emotional significance because speech is absent.Chomet, S. (Director). (2003).

In The Red Turtle, directed by Michael Dudok de Wit, natural sounds become emotional indicators of the protagonist's inner state. Nature itself functions as a silent narrator.

5. Sound Design and the Aesthetics of Silence

5.1 Silence and Ambient Sound

Absolute silence rarely exists in cinema. Filmmakers instead construct "perceived silence" by removing dialogue and music while preserving subtle environmental sounds. This selective reduction heightens sensory awareness.

In Wall-E, directed by Andrew Stanton, mechanical sounds replace traditional dialogue. Small auditory details such as rustling debris, electronic beeps, and distant wind create emotional loneliness and audience empathy toward the robot protagonist.

5.2 Silence as Contrast

Silence becomes particularly powerful when contrasted against chaotic or loud scenes. Abrupt silence following destruction or conflict often creates shock and emotional gravity.

In Grave of the Fireflies directed by Isao Takahata, silence following bombing sequences intensifies themes of trauma and helplessness. The absence of sound reflects emotional numbness and the inability of language to fully express suffering.

This approach aligns with trauma theory in cinema, where silence represents experiences beyond verbal articulation.

6. Case Studies

6.1 Case Study: Wall-E (2008)

WALL-E, produced by Pixar Animation Studios, is one of the strongest examples of silent storytelling in modern animation.

The film's first act contains very limited dialogue and instead relies upon visual storytelling, environmental design, and sound effects. WALL-E's binocular-like eyes communicate curiosity, affection, loneliness, and sadness without verbal explanation.

Silence in the film reflects both emotional emptiness and environmental devastation, reinforcing ecological themes while deepening audience empathy.

Film critic Roger Ebert praised the film for communicating "through images and emotions rather than words."

6.2 Case Study: The Red Turtle (2016)

The Red Turtle, co-produced by Studio Ghibli, is almost entirely wordless.

The film explores survival, mortality, coexistence, and harmony with nature through silence and environmental sound. The absence of dialogue allows audiences to interpret symbolism independently while enhancing emotional universality.

Its minimalist storytelling reflects Japanese aesthetic traditions, emphasizing contemplation and simplicity.

6.3 Case Study: Spirited Away (2001)

Spirited Away uses silence to construct emotional introspection and atmospheric immersion.

The train journey scene stands as one of animation cinema's most celebrated silent sequences. Chihiro silently observes flooded landscapes while ambient sound and restrained music create emotional depth.

Silence in the film symbolizes transition, maturity, and emotional self-awareness.

6.4 Case Study: Grave of the Fireflies (1988)

Grave of the Fireflies portrays the devastating realities of war through restrained storytelling and strategic silence.

Silent intervals following scenes of destruction force audiences to confront emotional trauma directly. Silence becomes a representation of grief, helplessness, and psychological devastation.

The film avoids melodramatic excess and instead achieves emotional realism through minimalism.

6.5 Case Study: The Triplets of Belleville (2003)

The Triplets of Belleville combines surrealism, visual humor, and minimal dialogue.

The film recalls traditions of silent cinema associated with Charlie Chaplin and Jacques Tati.

Silence enhances visual comedy, eccentric character design, and rhythmic movement while allowing humour to emerge visually rather than linguistically.

7. Cultural Perspectives on Silence in Animation

The use of silence differs significantly across cultural traditions.

Japanese Animation: Influenced by Zen Buddhism and traditional Japanese aesthetics, it often uses silence to evoke contemplation, harmony, and emotional subtlety.

Western Animation: Mainstream Hollywood animation traditionally emphasizes dialogue and musical continuity; however, films like Wall-E increasingly adopt silent storytelling techniques.

European Animation: European animated cinema frequently embraces minimal dialogue and artistic abstraction, prioritizing visual storytelling over verbal exposition.

These variations demonstrate that silence reflects broader artistic and philosophical values rather than merely technical choices.

8. Technological Evolution and Silence

Advancements in digital animation technology have expanded opportunities for silent storytelling.

Contemporary animation enables greater control over:

Subtle facial expressions

Environmental atmosphere

Lighting and texture

Ambient sound precision

Cinematic pacing

Emerging technologies such as Virtual Reality (VR), Augmented Reality (AR), and Artificial Intelligence (AI)-driven storytelling may further transform audience experiences of silence within immersive animated environments.

9. Conclusion

Silence in animation films represents far more than the absence of sound. It functions as a sophisticated cinematic language capable of expressing emotion, shaping narrative structure, and deepening audience engagement.

The analysis of films such as Wall-E, The Red Turtle, Spirited Away, Grave of the Fireflies, and The Triplets of Belleville demonstrates that silence can function simultaneously as a narrative device, a psychological instrument, an aesthetic strategy, and a philosophical statement.

Animation, because of its highly visual nature, is uniquely suited to silent storytelling. Through gestures, rhythm, composition, colour, and movement, animators communicate emotional depth beyond spoken language. Silence also strengthens universal accessibility by transcending linguistic barriers.

In contemporary media culture dominated by noise and constant communication, silence in animation offers viewers a contemplative alternative that restores emotional sensitivity and reflective engagement.

10. Future Scope

Future research on silence in animation may focus on:

- **Cross-Cultural Comparative Studies**

Comparative analysis of Eastern and Western uses of silence in animation.

- **Psychological Research**

Audience empathy, memory retention, and emotional processing in silent animated sequences.

- **Educational Animation**

Use of minimal-verbal animation for immersive educational learning.

- **Virtual Reality and Immersive Storytelling**

Silence in VR-based animation environments.

- **Animation Therapy and Mental Health**

Therapeutic applications of silent animation in trauma recovery and autism communication studies.

- **Artificial Intelligence and Interactive Media**

Adaptive silent storytelling generated dynamically through AI systems.

- **Environmental Storytelling**

Eco-critical studies examining silence and ecological consciousness in animation cinema.

References

- Bordwell, D., & Thompson, K. (2019). *Film Art: An Introduction* (12th ed.). McGraw-Hill Education.
- Chion, M. (1994). *Audio-Vision: Sound on Screen*. Columbia University Press.
- Wells, P. (1998). *Understanding Animation*. Routledge.
- Prince, S. (2012). *Movies and Meaning: An Introduction to Film*. Pearson Education.
- Eisenstein, S. (1949). *Film Form: Essays in Film Theory*. Harcourt Brace.
- Metz, C. (1974). *Film Language: A Semiotics of the Cinema*. University of Chicago Press.
- Arnheim, R. (1957). *Film as Art*. University of California Press.
- Manovich, L. (2001). *The Language of New Media*. MIT Press.

- Giannetti, L. (2014). *Understanding Movies* (13th ed.). Pearson.
- Chomet, S. (Director). (2003). *The Triplets of Belleville* [Film]. Les Armateurs.
- Dudok de Wit, M. (Director). (2016). *The Red Turtle* [Film]. Studio Ghibli & Wild Bunch.
- Miyazaki, H. (Director). (2001). *Spirited Away* [Film]. Studio Ghibli.
- Stanton, A. (Director). (2008). *Wall-E* [Film]. Pixar Animation Studios.
- Takahata, I. (Director). (1988). *Grave of the Fireflies* [Film]. Studio Ghibli.
- Ebert, R. (2008). Review of *Wall-E*. *Chicago Sun-Times*.
- Furniss, M. (2007). *Art in Motion: Animation Aesthetics*. Indiana University Press.
- Thomas, F., & Johnston, O. (1981). *The Illusion of Life: Disney Animation*. Disney Editions.
- McCloud, S. (1993). *Understanding Comics: The Invisible Art*. HarperCollins.
- Sito, T. (2013). *Moving Innovation: A History of Computer Animation*. MIT Press.
- Lamarre, T. (2009). *The Anime Machine: A Media Theory of Animation*. University of Minnesota Press.

End Notes

1. Michel Chion's theory suggests that cinematic silence is always perceived relative to surrounding sound.
2. The Japanese aesthetic concept of "ma" significantly influences silence in Studio Ghibli films.
3. Silent storytelling techniques in animation derive from silent cinema and pantomime traditions.
4. Environmental sounds within silent sequences often function symbolically.
5. Silence enhances universal accessibility by transcending language barriers.
6. Future immersive technologies may redefine audience experiences of silence in animated storytelling.

CHAPTER 9

Who Are the Real Watchdogs? Rhetorical Self-positioning of Digital-Native News Platforms in India

V Aswin and M Srihari

Abstract: Subscription and membership appeals of digital-native news outlets function not merely as requests for financial support. They are rhetorical and meta-journalistic sites through which media organisations attempt to represent their identity, values, vision and public purpose. In India's evolving media landscape, where press freedom and editorial independence are often contested, digital-native outlets have positioned themselves as alternatives to mainstream media. This chapter analyses the support/membership webpages and embedded promotional videos of three prominent digital-native news outlets: Newslaundry, Scroll and The Wire. These appeals provide an empirical lens through which to examine the construction of journalistic legitimacy. Drawing on Aristotle's concepts of ethos, pathos and logos alongside the Guard Dog perspective on media roles, it employs a two-tier coding framework to examine both the rhetorical strategies of persuasion and the positioning claims directed at the self and the mainstream media. Based on 42 coded excerpts, the findings reveal that ethos is the most frequently employed and dominant appeal followed by logos and then pathos, a pattern that differs from conventional advertising practices. Independence emerges as the central self-claim, while other-claims portray mainstream media as commercially captured, politically and editorially compromised. Through rhetoric, the platforms establish credibility and position themselves as alternative watchdogs, presenting reader-funding as both a basis for editorial independence and civic-duty. At the same time, the Guard Dog perspective brings a constitutive tension within this central claim, challenging the watchdog identity advanced by these outlets. The analysis contributes to broader debates on the journalistic legitimacy within the constantly evolving Indian media ecosystem.

Keywords: *Subscription Appeals, Rhetorical Analysis, Digital-Native Media, Guard Dog Model, Self-Positioning*

1. Introduction

The term digital-native is used in existing digital journalism scholarship to refer to news organisations that originated on digital platforms rather than transitioning from a legacy print or broadcast base (Nee, 2013). The distinction is significant because these organisations do not inherit any institutional infrastructure or established revenue streams. Consequently, subscription and membership appeals of digital-native news media cannot be regarded as ordinary buy/sell advertisements but persuasive narratives that ask readers to recognise the necessity of sustaining quality and independent journalism (Antonopoulos et al., 2020). They also constitute a form of meta journalistic discourse through which journalism defines and defends itself (Carlson, 2016).

When a digital-native news platform asks readers to pay for its journalism, it does considerably more than solicit money. In the act of explaining why it deserves support, a platform must state what kind of journalism it does, how that journalism differs from what is freely available elsewhere, and what is being challenged when the appeal goes unanswered. Digital-native media intervene and claim themselves as a refuge for the watchdog function (Harlow, 2022). This self-defining function acquires particular weight in the Indian mediascape where the financial and editorial independence of the mainstream press is widely contested (Chadha, 2017).

This chapter analyses the contents appearing on the dedicated support webpages of three prominent Indian digital-native news platforms: Newslaundry, Scroll.in and The Wire. These platforms position themselves as watchdogs of power adhering to the premise that whoever pays for news shapes its direction. So, the logic of patronage is not dissolved but has been relocated towards readers. The chapter aims to examine the rhetorical strategies used in their appeals and the claims the platforms make about themselves and the mainstream media. In doing so, it explores how the watchdog identity is constructed and the tensions that arise from the platform's own funding logic.

Digital-Native News Media in India:

Independent media is generally understood as institutions that maintain editorial autonomy free from the influence of government, corporations or other dominant power groups. But the term 'Independent media' itself remains a contested category (Bennett, 2014). They are also sometimes described as non-legacy media as they lack historical ties to established media organisations (Kling et al., 2025). It's been observed that such start-ups share three key characteristics: they are journalistic in nature, digitally native, and independent of legacy media organisations (Bruno & Nielsen, 2012). These characteristics are evident in the Indian platforms examined in this study and, this chapter prefers 'digital-native news outlets' to refer to its objects of study. Independence is understood as a claim that the platforms make about themselves but not as a fixed category to which they automatically belong. The rhetorical construction of that claim forms the focus of this chapter.

The growth of these platforms reflects a wider entrepreneurial turn in which journalists reframe precarity as an opportunity to reinvent journalism as both socially relevant and viable (Cohen, 2015; Usher, 2017). The formal consolidation of this sector is evident in the founding of the DIGIPUB News India Foundation in 2020 and its recognition as a Level II self-regulatory body in 2022. It asserts that the interests of digital-only media diverge from those of legacy media in regulation, business models and structure. The choice of subscription model is central to this self-understanding: by reducing reliance on advertising, reader funding is presented as a way to "serve the audience first" (*Reuters Digital News Report*, 2023).

2. Conceptual Framework

Aristotle defines Rhetoric as the faculty of observing the available means of persuasion in any given case. The class triad of ethos, logos and pathos work altogether to shape audience perception. Ethos foregrounds the source's character and authority, logos builds rational argument and pathos evokes emotional response (Aristotle & Kennedy, 2006). Since the subscription appeals are inherently persuasive, the triad offers a natural lens for examining how platforms build credibility, appeal to reader's emotions and justify the support they seek (Perloff, 2016).

The triad explains only how persuasion operates and not the specific claims that platforms make about themselves and their competitors. To address this, the chapter incorporates a second analytical framework based on the Guard Dog perspective on media roles. This perspective identifies four models of media behaviour: the watchdog model, which serves the public interest and challenges power; the lapdog model, which remains submissive to power; the oligarchy model, in which media form part of the power structure; and the guard dog model, in which media protect the interests of powerful groups (Donohue et al., 1995). Together, these models make it possible to examine support appeals not simply as fundraising messages but as efforts to define journalistic identity.

This produces a two-tier coding framework. Tier 1 records the dominant rhetorical mechanism (ethos, logos or pathos) and Tier 2 records the positioning claims made by the platform. These include self-claims, which refer to how the platform presents itself and other-claims, which refer to how it portrays mainstream media. These claims are then analysed in relation to the four media-role models. The two tiers of the framework are summarised below.

Tier	Codes
Tier 1: Rhetorical Mechanism	Ethos (awards, track record, named endorsers, independence, transparency), Pathos (civic-duty, community, shared struggle, calls to action, reader agency), Logos (cause-effect funding arguments, model explanation, facts and figures)
Tier 2: Self-claim	Independence, Credibility, Public Service, Community, Transparency, Courage. (Derived from the watchdog model)
Tier 2: Other-claim (On mainstream media)	Captured by commerce, Captured by power/state, Cowardly/timid, Negligent, False objectivity, Propaganda, Platform/algorithm dependence (Derived from the

	lapdog, oligarchy and guard-dog models)

3. Data and Methods:

The following selection of platforms was purposive: Newslaundry (Founded in 2012), Scroll (2014) and The Wire (2015). Each is well recognised, published principally in English, was launched within the past decade and relies substantially on reader funding rather than advertising. Newslaundry currently offers only a joint subscription along with The News Minute (2014), which focus on the coverage of Southern India. Scroll.in has adopted a membership model in which readers choose the amount thcy wish to contribute, while The Wire seeks tax-deductible donations for the Foundation for Independent Journalism under Section 80G. The shift from a transactional subscription model to membership and donation-based support is also rhetorically significant.

Data were drawn from each platform's support/membership webpage, accessed in May 2026, along with the promotional videos embedded on those pages. Inclusion of the videos in the analysis is important because they provide complementary information and perspective that is not available in the webpage text alone. The founder's spoken message (as in The Wire) and endorsements by public figures (as in Scroll) reveal a distinct rhetorical strategy in which criticism of mainstream media is expressed even through third-party voices.

The corpus comprises 42 coded excerpts including 24 from page text and 18 from video transcripts. Coding followed a directed, abductive procedure, with the codebook refined throughout the analysis. The codes should therefore be understood as provisional rather than foxed. Each excerpt was assigned a dominant Tier 1 rhetorical appeal and the relevant Tier 2 self-claims and other-claims. These claims were then analysed in relation to the four media-role models.

4. The Mechanics of Persuasion

Across the corpus, ethos emerged as the most frequently occurring dominant appeal (17 of 42 excerpts), followed by logos (15 excerpts) and pathos (10 excerpts). This pattern is significant because it differs from conventional advertising where emotional appeals often play a dominant role (Eckler, 2011). In the present corpus, credibility and rational argument are more prominent. This suggests that these platforms seek to persuade readers primarily by establishing the trustworthiness of their journalism and by presenting reader funding as a reasonable and necessary means of sustaining it. Although pathos is also present, it typically appears alongside ethos and logos and is often used to reinforce appeals for civic engagement and support.

Ethos is constructed through references to journalistic achievements, organisational longevity, awards and the authority of recognised individuals. Examples include Newslaundry's team videos, Scroll's use of endorsements from public intellectuals and direct appeals by The Wire's founder. Logos is evident in recurring arguments that connect reader funding with editorial independence, as well as in references to subscription plans, payment options and indicators such as the decline of press freedom index in India. Pathos is primarily expressed through appeals to community, shared responsibility and civic participation. Readers are addressed not as passive consumers but as members of a broader public who have a role in supporting independent journalism.

5. Independence as the Central Self claim

Among the self-claims identified in the corpus, independence appears most frequently (22 of 42 excerpts). It is followed by credibility and courage (10 excerpts each), public service (9), community (7) and transparency (3). The prominence of independence suggests that it functions as a central element in the watchdog identity constructed by these platforms. Newslaundry's statement, "We serve you, not the advertisers", draws a clear distinction between reader-supported and advertiser-supported journalism. Its videos further argue that reader funding enables fearless reporting by reducing dependence on corporate and political interests. Similarly, The Wire presents editorial and financial independence as essential conditions for quality journalism. Scroll.in emphasises independence through its "No ads" membership model and its commitment to focusing on stories it considers important.

Claims related to courage and public service are frequently supported through references to past journalistic work. Newslaundry highlights investigations such as Hathras, the Delhi Riots and "Who Owns Your Media" as examples of the outcomes made possible through reader funding. Scroll points to its reporting on issues related to land, gender and marginalised communities. While The Wire emphasizes its record of "fearless journalism" over the past decade. Transparency appears less frequently than other self-claims but remains note-worthy. Newslaundry explicitly rejects the ideal of complete objectivity, describing it as unattainable and invites readers to hold the organisation accountable. This represents an unusual form of reflexivity in which a platform that positions itself as a watchdog also presents itself as open to public scrutiny.

6. Critiquing the Mainstream Media

Self-positioining is shaped not only by claims about the self but also by criticisms aimed at the mainstream media. The most common other-claim in the corpus concerns commercial dependence. Mainstream media are frequently portrayed as being influenced by advertisers and commercial interests. Newslaundry, for instance, argues that journalism has been sacrificed "at the altar of clicks and TRPs". Such claims align with the oligarchy and guard dog models, in which media organisations are understood to serve the interests of those who finance or control them rather than the public.

A second set of other-claims focuses on political influence and pressure from the powerful actors. Scroll's references to journalists who are imprisoned and declining press freedom suggest a mediascape in which journalists face constraints on their independence. The Wire expresses this critique most directly by emphasizing the importance of asking questions that those in power would prefer to avoid. In doing so, it presents itself as a watchdog while implying that sections of the mainstream media have become reluctant to challenge power.

Other-claims also portray mainstream media as neglecting important issues, promoting false sense of objectivity or contributing to the spread of propaganda. Several examples suggest that mainstream outlets ignore significant stories or prioritise superficial content over public-interest reporting. One of Scroll's endorsers praises the platform for maintaining a commitment to truth at a time when the distinction between information and propaganda is becoming increasingly unclear. Another notable claim appears in Scroll's FAQ section, which argues that advertising revenue has become less reliable because the distribution of news is increasingly shaped by social media platforms and search-engine algorithms. This extends the critique beyond advertisers to the digital infrastructures that influence the visibility and circulation of news.

The promotional videos reveal an additional rhetorical strategy. Criticism of mainstream media is often voiced by third parties, including public intellectuals, public figures and platform founders. By presenting these criticisms through external voices, the platforms strengthen the credibility of their claims and reduce the self-promotion perspective. For instance, the claim that Scroll's reporting on the Adani group represents some of its most courageous journalism gains additional persuasive force when it is made by an endorser rather than by the platform itself.

7. The Watchdog Positioning

Across the corpus, the three platforms converge on a coherent self-positioning. Ethos asserts credibility, logos ties reader funding to editorial freedom and pathos appeals payment as a civic duty. This places them within the normative position that has been found most effective in encouraging readers to pay for news (Wilczek et al., 2023). The current analysis confirms that finding in a non-western setting. While existing reader-revenue appeals align with informational, social and normative forms (Nechushtai & Zalmanson, 2021), the Indian case highlights a dimension that these categories do not fully capture; that is the sustained boundary work against a delegitimised and partisan mainstream. The other-claims identified in Tier 2 are not incidental but constitutive of the observation. These appeals can be understood as meta-journalistic sites at which boundaries of "real" journalism are defined and mainstream media are positioned firmly outside them (Carlson, 2016).

The boundary work also reflects the founder identities as described in the study of Harlow & Chadha (2018). They classify Newslaundry founders as "Guardians", who are characterised by the dissatisfaction with mainstream media and are committed to building a better alternative. The platform's subscription appeals explicitly reflect the same dimension. In this sense, the actor-level orientation as informed by the existing scholarship extends into the outlet's textual self-representation. The prominence of other-claims is also consistent with evidence that willingness to pay for news increases with awareness of the problems faced by the industry (Newman et al., 2018). By foregrounding the mainstream's capture, negligence and timidity, the platforms do not merely contrast themselves with them, but also actively cultivate the problem-awareness that the literature associates with paying readers, manufacturing the condition their appeals depend upon.

The Guard Dog model was developed to describe media organisations that serve the interests of the powerful groups that fund and control them (Donohue et al., 1995). Reader-funded journalism is often presented as an alternative to this arrangement. Yet the platform's own central premise, that those who pay for news determine its direction, appears to reproduce a part of the same logic. If payment shapes the direction, reader funding does not avoid sponsorship but rather disperses the funding across sponsorship. The watchdog claim is therefore advanced through the very mechanism that has the potential to compromise it in the guard-dog model. In this sense, the chapter's framing question exposes a tension already embedded within the guard-dog model.

Reading the appeals alongside the Guard-dog framework allows the model to be examined under funding conditions that its authors did not anticipate. The analysis suggests that elements of the guard-dog logic persist even when elite sponsors are replaced by readers. At the same time, the appeals attempt to address this tension rhetorically. The Wire describes its supporters as people who have "no interest other than to sustain a space for quality journalism", while Newslaundry argues that "when public pays, the public is served". In both cases, the sponsor is represented as an unbiased supporter of journalism rather than as an actor seeking influence. The shift towards membership and donation models further reinforces this framing by presenting financial support as a civic contribution without editorial stake.

The brand identity appeals, generally relying on ethos and logos, are considered least effective to promote engagement and the emotional tone is generally regarded as the stronger driver instead (Collier et al., 2021; Eckler & Bolls, 2011). The analysed corpus reveals the platform's emphasis on credibility and rational argument. This reflects the identities they seek to represent as independence, rigour and watchdog mission rather than a strategic alignment that would encourage payment. The three platforms express this shared position in different ways. Newslaundry employs the most multimedia-rich and reflexive appeal, even asking readers to scrutinise its own practices. Scroll combines logical and emotional appeals while openly retaining advertising for non-members. The Wire advances the most explicit narrative of presenting themselves as a challenger to the established media order. Despite these differences, all three platforms construct a watchdog identity grounded in reader funding. The common underlying logic is that reader-supported journalism brings independence and autonomy, even though the same funding logic introduces a potential tension as informed by the Guard-dog model. Essentially, this conclusion is concerned with the rhetoric of the appeals rather than newsroom practice or content analysis which lies beyond the scope of the present analysis.

8. Conclusion

Digital-native news outlets in India use credibility, rational argument and emotional appeals to encourage readers to become monetary contributors. In doing so, they also position themselves as alternative watchdogs in contrast to a mainstream media landscape portrayed as influenced by advertisers and power groups. The two-tier framework reveals that this positioning is constructed not only through self-claims but also through claims about mainstream media aimed at critiquing its obvious structural foundations. The appeals are persuasive and internally consistent on their own terms. The watchdog identity claimed by these platforms' rests on the argument that funding influences the editorial direction. Read against the guard dog perspective, the very same premise of independence through reader donations is being challenged. The shift from subscription models towards membership and donation-based support can therefore be interpreted as an effort to manage this tension by presenting readers as disinterested supporters of journalism rather than as sponsors with particular interests and orientations. The orientation of the outlets in practice, need to be investigated through further studies as that lies beyond the scope of the current analysis. The subscription appeals project the sector as seeking to establish and maintain a watchdog identity under conditions of declining press freedom and continuing uncertainty about sustainable funding models for digital journalism.

References

- Antonopoulos, N., Lamprou, E., Kiourexidou, M., Konidaris, A., & Polykalas, S. (2020). Media websites services and users subscription models for online journalism. *Media Watch, 11*(2), 310–322. https://doi.org/10.15655/mw_2020_v11i2_195650

- Aristotle. (2006). *On rhetoric: A theory of civic discourse* (G. A. Kennedy, Trans., 2nd ed.). Oxford University Press.

- Bennett, J. (2014). Introduction: The utopia of independent media: Independence, working with freedom and working for free. In *Media independence: Working with freedom or working for free?* (pp. 1–18). Routledge.

- Bruno, N., & Nielsen, R. K. (2012). *Survival is success: Journalistic online start-ups in Western Europe*. Reuters Institute for the Study of Journalism.

- Carlson, M. (2016). Metajournalistic discourse and the meanings of journalism: Definitional control, boundary work, and legitimation. *Communication Theory, 26*(4), 349–368. https://doi.org/10.1111/comt.12088

- Chadha, K. (2017). The Indian news media industry: Structural trends and journalistic implications. *Global Media and Communication, 13*(2), 139–156. https://doi.org/10.1177/1742766517704674

- Cohen, N. S. (2015). Entrepreneurial journalism and the precarious state of media work. *South Atlantic Quarterly, 114*(3), 513–533. https://doi.org/10.1215/00382876-3130723

- Collier, J., Kim, Y., & Stroud, N. J. (2021). How news images affect clicking on subscription appeals. *Journalism Practice, 15*(4), 489–507. https://doi.org/10.1080/17512786.2020.1738262

- Donohue, G. A., Tichenor, P. J., & Olien, C. N. (1995). A guard dog perspective on the role of media. *Journal of Communication, 45*(2), 115–132. https://doi.org/10.1111/j.1460-2466.1995.tb00732.x

- Eckler, P., & Bolls, P. D. (2011). Spreading the virus: Emotional tone of viral advertising and its effect on forwarding intentions and attitudes. *Journal of Interactive Advertising, 11*(2), 1–11. https://doi.org/10.1080/15252019.2011.10722180

- Harlow, S. (2022). A new people's press? Understanding digital-native news sites in Latin America as alternative media. *Digital Journalism, 10*(8), 1322–1341. https://doi.org/10.1080/21670811.2021.1907204

- Harlow, S., & Chadha, M. (2019). Indian entrepreneurial journalism. *Journalism Studies, 20*(6), 835–856. https://doi.org/10.1080/1461670X.2018.1463170

- Kling, J., Toepfl, F., & Jürgens, P. (2025). Entertainment interspersed with propaganda: How non-legacy-news accounts deliver explicitly political content to mass audiences on Russia's most popular social network VK. *Information, Communication & Society, 28*(7), 1252–1269. https://doi.org/10.1080/1369118X.2024.2420029

- Nechushtai, E., & Zalmanson, L. (2021). "Stay informed," "become an insider" or "drive change": Repackaging newspaper subscriptions in the digital age. *Journalism, 22*(8), 2035–2052. https://doi.org/10.1177/1464884919847350

- Nee, R. C. (2013). Creative destruction: An exploratory study of how digitally native news nonprofits are innovating online journalism practices. *International Journal on Media Management, 15*(1), 3–22. https://doi.org/10.1080/14241277.2012.732153

- Newman, N., Fletcher, R., Kalogeropoulos, A., & Levy, D. A. L. (2018). *Reuters Institute digital news report 2018*. Reuters Institute for the Study of Journalism.
- Perloff, R. M. (2016). *The dynamics of persuasion: Communication and attitudes in the twenty-first century* (6th ed.). Routledge. https://doi.org/10.4324/9781315657714
- Reuters Institute for the Study of Journalism. (2023). *Digital news report 2023*. University of Oxford. https://reutersinstitute.politics.ox.ac.uk/digital-news-report/2023
- Usher, N. (2017). Venture-backed news startups and the field of journalism: Challenges, changes, and consistencies. *Digital Journalism, 5*(9), 1116–1133. https://doi.org/10.1080/21670811.2016.1272064
- Wilczek, B., Schulte-Uentrop, I., & Thurman, N. (2023). Subscribe now: On the effectiveness of advertising messages in promoting newspapers' online subscriptions. *International Journal of Communication, 17*, 3461–3483.